AMERICA'S NEXT top model™

FACE VALUE

Read all the books in the

AMERICA'S NEXT top model™ Series:

1: Face Value

2: Eye Candy

AMERICA'S NEXT top model™

FACE VALUE

Taryn Bell

Scholastic Inc.
New York Toronto London Auckland
Sydney Mexico City New Delhi Hong Kong

Published by Scholastic Inc. SCHOLASTIC and associated logos are trademarks and/or registered trademarks of Scholastic Inc.

ISBN-13: 978-0-545-14111-6
ISBN-10: 0-545-14111-7

12 11 10 9 8 7 6 5 4 3 2 1   9 10 11 12 13 14/0

Printed in the U.S.A.
First edition, August 2009

TOP MODEL
PREPARATORY
SUMMER PROGRAM
A DIVISION OF
AMERICA'S NEXT TOP
MODEL AGENCY, INC.

235 Spring Street
New York, NY 10012

Dear Top Model Prep applicant:

Have you always wanted to be a model? Are you ready for the most fabulous summer of your life?

Top Model Prep's summer program will be the stepping-stone to success beyond your wildest dreams.

Top Model Prep is owned and operated by the prestigious America's Next Top Model Agency, Inc., which was founded on the success of the wildly popular television show of the same name. Our headmistress, Victoria Devachan, was, of course, one of the most famous supermodels of her time.

We are located in New York City, the fashion and modeling capital of the world. Accepted students will live, four to an apartment, in the Top Model Residence, a state-of-the-art building in SoHo. The selected young women will spend eight exciting weeks accepting challenges, overcoming obstacles, and finding out if they have what it takes to make it as a supermodel.

Please answer all questions and include three recent photos, a copy of your grades, and a letter from your parent or guardian.

TOP MODEL PREPARATORY SUMMER PROGRAM
A DIVISION OF AMERICA'S NEXT TOP MODEL AGENCY, INC.

Applicant #1

NAME: *ALEXIS COURNOS*

AGE: *16*

HOMETOWN: *Detroit, MI*

SCHOOL/GPA: *Hamtramck High School, B- average*

WHAT DO YOU SEE WHEN YOU LOOK IN THE MIRROR?
I am energetic, curious, and fun-loving.

WHY DO YOU WANT TO ATTEND TOP MODEL PREP?
It's the adventure of a lifetime! I am all about widening my horizons, meeting new people, and I've always wanted to go to New York City.

WHY SHOULD WE CONSIDER YOU?
Because I'm up for anything! Makeover? Cool! Shave my head? Bring it!

WHAT WILL YOU BE GIVING UP TO SPEND THE SUMMER AT TOP MODEL PREP?
Nothing! It's all good!

WHAT DO YOU CONSIDER YOUR GREATEST STRENGTH?
My ability to portray different emotions on camera.

WHAT'S A PERSONAL WEAKNESS OR FLAW?
I've been told that I'm too impulsive.

WHAT IS YOUR ULTIMATE GOAL?
To travel around the world, have new experiences, and meet cool people!! And I wouldn't mind dating a male model (LOL!)

------------ Do Not Write Below This Line ------------

Administration Comments:

Victoria Devachan — Headmistress:
Her overuse of ! should be a clue! She may be too much of a good thing. And yet, there's something infectious about her (let's hope it's not toxic).

Recommendation:
Admit with caution.

Anabelle Trembley — stylist, designer, visionary:
Alexis is blessed with an oval face, green/blue eyes, and wild ginger hair—she's a modern day Greek goddess. She radiates light, and such positivity!

Recommendation:
Admit!

Dan'yel Fieldstone — makeup artist, creative director:
Alexis is underheight and overenthusiastic. Wild streak. A firecracker. Most likely to explode—and get everyone else into trouble while she's at it.

Recommendation:
What are we deliberating about? Light the fuse!

TOP MODEL PREPARATORY SUMMER PROGRAM
A DIVISION OF AMERICA'S NEXT TOP MODEL AGENCY, INC.

Applicant #2

NAME: *CHLOE HUNTLEY*

AGE: *16*

HOMETOWN: *Los Angeles, CA*

SCHOOL/GPA: *Crossroads Academy in Santa Monica. We don't do grades at my school.*

WHAT DO YOU SEE WHEN YOU LOOK IN THE MIRROR?
A younger version of my mother.

WHY DO YOU WANT TO ATTEND TOP MODEL PREP?
I've been expected to attend since I was in diapers.

WHY SHOULD WE CONSIDER YOU?
I am Charlotte Huntley's daughter. My grandmother (as you no doubt know) modeled alongside Audrey Hepburn, and my great-grandmother was the original waif-model in the 1930s.

WHAT WILL YOU BE GIVING UP TO SPEND THE SUMMER AT TOP MODEL PREP?
My boyfriend, but I'm hoping to see him on weekends.

WHAT DO YOU CONSIDER YOUR GREATEST STRENGTH?
My talent for writing poetry. I mean, my ability to photograph well.

WHAT'S A PERSONAL WEAKNESS OR FLAW?
My eyebrows benefit from special waxing. Because I am naturally pale, tanning is crucial—all of which I assume is provided at TMP.

WHAT IS YOUR ULTIMATE GOAL?
I'm not sure. . . .

------------ Do Not Write Below This Line ------------

Administration Comments:

Victoria Devachan — Headmistress:
Chloe is a legacy. Charlotte wants her here.

Recommendation:
Admit ASAP! And please see that her housing accommodations are acceptable to Charlotte.

Anabelle Trembley — stylist, designer, visionary:
Chloe has platinum hair, porcelain skin, pale blue eyes, long legs, and a slim figure. Modeling is her destiny.

Recommendation:
Admit!!

Dan'yel Fieldstone — makeup artist, creative director:
She doesn't want to be here, yet she's modeling royalty. Her photos will kick butt. The others will hate her. Oh, and the boyfriend back home thing? That never works.

Recommendation:
There's a doubt? She's in!

TOP MODEL PREPARATORY SUMMER PROGRAM
A DIVISION OF AMERICA'S NEXT TOP MODEL AGENCY, INC.

Applicant #3:

NAME: *LINDSAY J. ROBINSON*

AGE: *16*

HOMETOWN: *Staten Island, New York, temporarily.*

SCHOOL/GPA: *Richmond High School. They give me Cs, but they're prejudiced against actors. Everyone knows it. So unfair!*

WHAT DO YOU SEE WHEN YOU LOOK IN THE MIRROR?
A caramel complexion, big brown eyes, full lips, hair that can go straight, wavy, or full-out curly, and a body that's curvy in the right places—know what I mean?

WHY DO YOU WANT TO ATTEND TOP MODEL PREP?
It's the next step in my career, which I can't WAIT to get back to!

WHY SHOULD WE CONSIDER YOU?
Maybe you remember me? I starred as D'Neese, the adorable niece on the TV show, Yes, We Blend. *You can see reruns on TBS because it's a classic. When I hit puberty—okay, fine, so I gained a little weight—LOL—they said my contract was up . . . (continued on back)*

WHAT WILL YOU BE GIVING UP TO SPEND THE SUMMER AT TOP MODEL PREP?
Oh, let's see . . . glamorous Staten Island? Proximity to landfills?

WHAT DO YOU CONSIDER YOUR GREATEST STRENGTH?
Star quality!

WHAT'S A PERSONAL WEAKNESS OR FLAW?
Probably I could stand to drop those last two lbs., and sometimes I get breakouts—but as we in the biz know, airbrushing, makeup, and the gym are a girl's best friends.

WHAT IS YOUR ULTIMATE GOAL?
Brandocity! Modeling will give me the comeback I need to launch myself to international stardom. I will have a fragrance, a clothing line, maybe a reality TV show, but I think that's so over. . . .
(continued on back)

------------ Do Not Write Below This Line ------------

Administration Comments:

Victoria Devachan—Headmistress:
Poor Lindsay, a has-been at sixteen, but a comeback story makes good copy. She'll bring great publicity to the school—unless she wins, of course.

Recommendation: Admit

Anabelle Trembley—stylist, designer, visionary:
Lindsay is like Beyoncé, in constant Sasha-Fierce mode.

Recommendation: Admit!!

Dan'yel Fieldstone—makeup artist, creative director:
Just because she used to be on TV, she thinks modeling will be a breeze. I predict an ill wind.

Recommendation: Blow on!

TOP MODEL
PREPARATORY
SUMMER PROGRAM
A DIVISION OF
AMERICA'S NEXT TOP
MODEL AGENCY, INC.

Applicant #4

NAME: *SHIVA-ROSE SAFIR*

AGE: *17*

HOMETOWN: *Haifa, Israel*

SCHOOL/GPA: *Bat Galim High School.*
My grades translate to straight As.

WHAT DO YOU SEE WHEN YOU LOOK IN THE MIRROR?
My friends say I look like Bar Rafaeli, the model who is Leonardo DiCaprio's girlfriend.

WHY DO YOU WANT TO ATTEND TOP MODEL PREP?
I think it will give the best possible direction for my future.

WHY SHOULD WE CONSIDER YOU?
I could be the next Victoria's Secret girl—you won't know until you try me!

WHAT WILL YOU BE GIVING UP TO SPEND THE SUMMER AT TOP MODEL PREP?
My last summer with some of my friends before they start in the army.

WHAT DO YOU CONSIDER YOUR GREATEST STRENGTH?
My shoulders?

WHAT'S A PERSONAL WEAKNESS OR FLAW?
My legs may be too skinny?

WHAT IS YOUR ULTIMATE GOAL?
To exceed the expectations of my family and succeed in this field. Otherwise, I want to attend the Technion Institute in Tel Aviv.

------------ Do Not Write Below This Line ------------

Administration Comments:

Victoria Devachan — Headmistress:
Diversity student and scholarship student = divine! With only one tuition for us to absorb.

Recommendation :
Send her admission by DHL; they deliver to that part of the world.

Anabelle Trembley — stylist, designer, visionary:
Shiva-Rose has sunbaked skin, dark eyes, and dark hair. She's our Middle Eastern princess. We can achieve world peace with Shiva-Rose.

Recommendation:
Shalom! (Welcome)

Dan'yel Fieldstone — makeup artist, creative director:
Glug. Glug. Glug. Gefilte fish out of the bathtub. She'll probably be a Holy, hot mess.

Recommendation:
And on the fifth day, I saith, Admit!

TOP MODEL
PREPARATORY
SUMMER PROGRAM
A DIVISION OF
AMERICA'S NEXT TOP
MODEL AGENCY, INC.

Schedule

Session One

July 1–July 15:
40 girls in competition; 10 eliminations post-challenge; 1 winner of challenge.

Session Two

July 16–July 31:
30 girls in competition; 10 eliminations; 1 winner of challenge.

Session Three

August 1–August 15; 20 girls in competition; 10 eliminations; 1 winner of challenge

Session Four

August 16–August 30: 10 girls in competition; 1 winner — America's Next Top Model!

Grand Prize:
The winner will receive a contract with our agency, America's Next Top Model Agency, Inc. She will appear on the cover of *Seventeen* magazine, along with a four-page fashion spread. She will also take home a check in the amount of $100,000, to be used toward her college education.

Good luck, and dream big!

Chapter One
Turf Wars

"Sa-*weet*!"

Alexis Helena Cournos dropped her backpack and sprinted into the sun-drenched, fourteenth-floor apartment, thrilled to be the first roommate to arrive. She could feel it in her bones: This summer would go down in Alexis-history as The. Coolest. Ever.

All she had to do was play by the rules—easier said than done.

She'd applied to Top Model Prep on a total lark, and hadn't expected to actually get in. Models were all about enigmatic beauty, sultriness, and allure. Alexis knew she was more the girl-next-door type: cute in a sunny-side-up, sparkly way.

But somehow she'd been accepted into the toughest modeling competition in the USA.

And now, on July first, here she was in New York City, one thousand miles, and a million already fading memories, away from boring Hamtramck,

Michigan. Alexis glanced out the window, down at the horn-honking yellow taxicabs gliding toward Broadway, at the hustle and bustle of fashionistas and hipsters streaming in and out of swanky boutiques. She couldn't believe she was a part of it, the world's biggest and coolest playground.

Alexis turned away from the window to continue her tour of the apartment. The common room was welcoming, with cushiony L-shaped couches and a nicked coffee table. The bathroom was all marble and ivory, with a humongous old-fashioned claw-foot bathtub. Alexis had only ever seen anything like it in pictures. In person, it beckoned her to strip down, turn on the gushing faucets, and jump in. She pictured herself under a down blanket of foaming bubbles, head tipped back, her long corkscrew curls draped over the bathtub rim. Her first modeling shoot! Maybe she'd suggest it to the photographers.

Alexis caught her reflection in the lighted mirror and laughed. Her tangled mop of strawberry frizz flew wild. Her freckles threatened a hostile takeover of her shoulders. Not such a model-worthy look. But as long as no one saw the word *imposter* stamped on her forehead, she'd be all right.

Feeling a nervous pang, Alexis wondered about her three roommates, who'd probably show up soon. She hoped at least one or two would be normal girls, not statuesque, perfect, privileged princesses who felt entitled to win (and probably were). Alexis swallowed hard. What if everyone was not only model-worthy, but model-stereotypical as well: dim, demanding, surly, petty, backstabbing, or morose? Not having a friend here would truly suck.

Whatever, since she was there and they weren't, Alexis figured she had dibs on beds.

There were two bedrooms. One was large, yellow, and square-shaped, arranged as a triple. It had a dorm room vibe, with a bunk bed hugging one wall and a single twin perpendicular to it. Three tall, narrow windows let in a lot of light, and there was an actual walk-in closet—she'd never been in one before!

The other bedroom was across from the common room. Smaller than the triple, it was gussied up (as her grandma would say) in shades of pinks and purples, with one duvet-covered bed, a desk, fringed lampshade, tallboy bureau, and closet. All the room needed was posters of kittens and daisies to remind Alexis of her girlie-girl bedroom from back home.

Alexis didn't need to deliberate. She claimed her space immediately.

What a dump.

Chloe Huntley had barely managed to drag her Louis Vuitton luggage into that claustrophobia-inducing, creaking elevator—no paying student, let alone next top model, should have been exposed to it—only to have to find her way here. Clearly, Suite 14C had long ago been an opulent apartment, but was now going for a shabby-chic dorm look, and only managing the shabby part.

She couldn't bring herself to investigate. It was bad enough being forced to breathe this stale, dank air in the aptly named "common" room. With its bad lighting, drab draperies, and ancient furniture, the place was in need of an interior designer or a wrecking ball, whichever could get there first. Why her mother had sent her three thousand miles and a bunch of time zones away from her actual life was a mystery. She was going to be a supermodel anyway, like it or not. That was a gimme.

Eight weeks of enforced detention, that's what

this summer felt like. Two months wasted in some smiley-face competition, dumped into a sea of wannabes most likely to be nobodies.

Dispirited, Chloe adjusted the hem of her Jason Wu minidress and dropped onto a saggy club chair. She promptly whipped out her iPhone and texted the love of her life, Liam Lattimore.

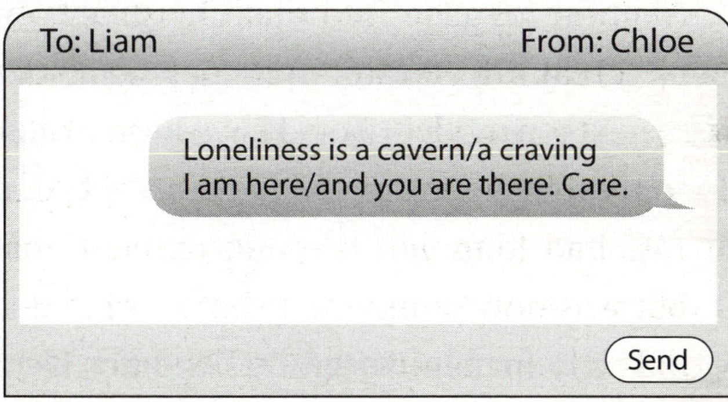

When texting with her back-home BFFs, Chloe was all about "OMG"s and "BTW"s. But Liam knew the *real* her.

With all the patience of a hummingbird on Red Bull, she kept looking for an instant response. None came.

She reminded herself that it was still early in California, especially for her boyfriend, who, on weekends, rarely stirred before the crack of noon. Plus, she knew that after Liam had driven her to the airport last night and kissed her good-bye, he'd gone with some of his buddies to The Kresse, the hottest club in LA. Just thinking about the bright lights of Sunset Boulevard made a wave of homesickness crash over Chloe.

"Hi there!"

Chloe gave a start and glanced up to see a freckled sprite hovering over her. Judging by her outfit—green Old Navy tank top, Gap jeans, flip-flops—it was clear that this wannabe competitor hailed from one of the flyover states. Still, nothing about her said "all-American girl." Her hair was carrot-colored, with glints of amber, her eyes flicked from blue to green. And her lashes, thick, long, and charcoal—the kind Chloe's friends dropped serious money on at Beverly Hills salons—were unsettlingly real.

"I was so busy getting unpacked, I didn't hear anyone come in," roommate-girl rambled on. "Isn't this place amazing? I'm Alexis, by the way. And you're—"

Underwhelmed. And miserable. Chloe masked her feelings behind her veneer-perfect smile, and tossed her gleaming blond locks over her shoulder.

"Chloe Huntley," she replied, bracing herself for Alexis's inevitable jaw-drop of recognition. But the other girl's expression remained blank, if still over-eager. Chloe felt a rush of relief. Alexis had no clue who Chloe was—or wasn't. In LA, people either thought she was a cast member from *The Hills*, or instantly realized that she was the exact replica of her mother, supermodel Charlotte Huntley.

"Where's your stuff?" Alexis asked, looking around.

"Outside." Chloe motioned toward the hallway. "I was about to drag it in."

"I'll help," Alexis offered.

Chloe gave a sigh, abandoning her iPhone on the chair along with the hope that Liam would wake up anytime soon. She rose up in her platform Stuart Weitzman slides, noticing right away how drastically under the modeling height requirement Alexis was. The girl had to be five-six on a really good Manolo day. Which meant that she'd probably be one of the ten hopefuls booted off in the first session, and therefore no competition at all to Chloe.

But do I even want to win? Chloe asked herself

before pushing the thought away and following Alexis to the door.

"I was told there was a single here," Chloe mentioned casually, hoping early-bird Alexis hadn't assumed the solo room would be hers.

"Go for it." Alexis pointed to the doorway on the other side of the common room. "I'm all about bunk beds. I took the top one!"

Good choice. Chloe smirked to herself. Alexis was probably the only one small enough to not bang her head on the ceiling when she sat upright.

"Excuse me, *what* is going on here?" Lindsay Robinson demanded, pausing at the entrance to the private room. She put one hand on the hip of her high-waisted gray trousers, into which she'd tucked a snug white tank top, the better to showcase her curves and cocoa-colored skin.

Lindsay was floored by the sight before her: a skinny Barbie type—*Chloe Huntley*, Lindsay realized, recognizing the girl's impeccable features from the pages of *Us Weekly*—was hanging up her designer clothes in the closet while her suitcases lay splayed open on the bed. Lindsay gritted her teeth. She had specifically asked Top

Model Prep for a single. That had been a non-negotiable.

"Um, can I help you?" Chloe asked coolly, scooping up a Michael Stars shrug from her suitcase.

"*Um*, yeah, you can," Lindsay snapped, tightening her slim silver headband over her puffy dark curls. "The private room is supposed to be mine."

Chloe blinked, then shook her head. "That can't be. The school pre-reserved this room for me. You'll be staying with Alexis in the triple."

Lindsay felt herself reddening. She inhaled a deep, three-part yoga breath and exhaled an Emmy-worthy performance of a reply. "Well, someone with actual on-camera experience requires more privacy. The school knows that."

There. With one sharp well-delivered quip, she'd put Chloe, "I'm Charlotte Huntley's look-alike daughter," in her place. She'd let her know that being a star—even a fading star—trumps being a model-spawn. So what if Chloe's mother had once been the world's biggest supermodel? *She* was Lindsay Robinson, and she wasn't sharing a room, let alone a triple!

"Ooh, what kind of on-camera experience? Like, commercials and stuff?" asked the bright-eyed redhead who suddenly cropped up next to Lindsay. *Alexis*, Lindsay guessed, trying not to roll her brown eyes.

Have you never watched TV? Lindsay wanted to bark. *What cave did you just crawl out of?*

"Whatever," Lindsay huffed instead, whipping her cell phone out of her Anya Hindmarch for Target clutch. "I'll take care of this. I'm calling Ms. Devachan and making sure I'm moved into my rightful spot."

"Ms. Devachan?" Chloe smiled smugly. "You mean Aunt Vickie? She and my mom have been friends for ages."

Lindsay sucked in a sharp breath, knowing that the model-spawn had played her trump card. Fine. Chloe may have won this battle, but she was going to lose the war.

Big-time.

Lindsay dropped her cell back in the clutch and turned on the chunky heel of her Baby Phat sandal. "Keep the lame room, then," she hissed over her shoulder. "It's not like I'll be spending that much time here anyway. I'll be taking meetings with my agents and going to parties with my friends."

"You mean you're *from* New York?" Alexis squealed, leading Lindsay through the common area. "That's ah-mazing! You have to show me around the city. . . ."

Lindsay let Alexis walk ahead and prattle on while she came to an abrupt stop, her attention diverted by something on a nearby chair. An iPhone. But whose? Could it belong to Chloe? Lindsay felt a prickle of excitement.

She'd been part of the "industry" long enough to know what winning was all about: ruthless manipulation and cunning. Which meant she had absolutely no qualms about reaching for the phone, ready to see what secrets—

"D'Neese?"

The iPhone slipped out of Lindsay's hand, dropping back onto the chair. She jerked her head up to see a dazzling, sun-streaked brunette with almond-shaped dark eyes standing in the doorway.

"That was your name, right?" the girl continued in a heavy Middle Eastern accent. "On the TV show?"

"Yeah, but it's Lindsay in real life," Lindsay muttered, half flattered and half annoyed that her little recon mission had been interrupted.

"I'm Shiva-Rose Safir," the girl said, dropping her camouflage duffel onto the floor. "From Haifa. Israel."

Isn't that peachy, Lindsay thought, scowling. *The only one who recognizes me isn't even from this country!*

"Wow," Shiva-Rose went on, walking over to Lindsay and beaming. "My first day in New York, and I've already met a star."

"A star?" Chloe echoed, popping her blond head out of the single room and looking confused.

"What? You don't know? She played D'Neese on *Yes, We Blend*!" Shiva-Rose gushed while Lindsay bristled.

Chloe's sky blue eyes widened. "OMG!" she exclaimed, "That was *you*? I'd never have guessed. You used to be adorable! What happened?"

Did she seriously just say that?

Lindsay balled her hands into fists, ready to snark back, when the iPhone on the chair let out a chirping sound. At the same instant, Lindsay felt her own cell phone buzz in her clutch while

Shiva-Rose dug into the pocket of her carpenter capri pants.

"Oh, *there's* my phone!" Chloe cried, rushing over and snatching up the iPhone. "I was looking for it all over. Hey, it's a text from Aunt Vickie!"

"Did you guys just get a text?" Alexis asked, barreling out of the triple with her cell phone held aloft.

Still vowing to exact revenge upon Chloe, Lindsay whipped out her cell and read the message that all the girls had received:

Welcome to Top Model Prep!
Meet me in an hour on the rooftop deck of SoHo House for poolside mocktails, hors d'oeuvres, and orientation.
And be ready to take NYC by storm!
xoxo
V

Chapter Two
On Top of the World

The rooftop of Soho House was bathed in an aura of pure white, sparkling blue, and elitism. Waitstaff roamed about, bearing trays of mocktinis and juicy bites of empanadas, spring rolls, sushi, and sashimi. Cushioned chaise lounges and tulle-tented cabanas ringed an iridescent blue swimming pool.

Shiva-Rose Safir lifted a HELLO MY NAME IS tag from the sign-in table and affixed it to her form-fitting white tee. Then she took a sip from the frothy, too-sweet pink drink a waiter had handed her, and surveyed her new surroundings. Back home in Haifa, she'd read about SoHo House, the exclusive hotel-slash-club, in fashion magazines, and had seen images of it on *Sex and the City* (she was a total TV addict). But she never thought she'd wind up here.

And as she watched the thirty-nine other giggling, squealing girls congregate around her, she couldn't have felt more different from them all. She overheard them making plans to see the city, meet boys, buy shoes. All of it seemed so trivial.

Just like her three roommates, who'd gotten so heated over which rooms they were staying in; as a result, the four of them had shared a tense, wordless cab ride to SoHo House.

Shiva-Rose didn't care where she roomed. She didn't care that she had to share a bunk bed with hyper Alexis, while moody Lindsay—whose fame still completely intimidated Shiva-Rose—seethed on the twin bed, and effortlessly gorgeous Chloe lived it up in the single.

She had other goals, other responsibilities.

She was here for one reason only: to win. If she could accumulate the necessary funds, she intended to go to a university and study science.

Alexis, the one roomie who seemed somewhat down-to-earth, sidled up next to Shiva-Rose, clutching an oversize patent leather tote like it was a life preserver. "Should we sit?" she offered cheerily, gesturing to the forty pristine white chairs that had been arranged before a giant plasma screen. Shots of high-fashion models and celebrities laughing, posing, and looking fabulous were playing across the screen on a constant loop.

Shiva-Rose glanced around; she saw Lindsay standing by the pool with her hands on her hips, her intelligent, critical gaze darting about. Chloe was chatting up a tall, chic, middle-aged woman with auburn curls whom Shiva-Rose recognized as none other than the headmistress, Victoria Devachan. The former supermodel was clad in a silk indigo pantsuit and sky-high heels, cutting a commanding figure.

"This sure feels different from home," Alexis commented breezily as she and Shiva-Rose sat down, drinks in hand.

The mention of home slit open a pit in Shiva-Rose's stomach. She hadn't expected to miss her dad, cousins, and especially her friends so soon. Ironically, if not for them, she wouldn't even be here. They were the ones who'd pushed her to apply to Top Model Prep after seeing the commercial on TV. Several Israeli and Middle Eastern girls had made it as supermodels, and lots of her friends wished they could, too. But everyone knew Shiva-Rose was the most likely.

Their opinion. Not hers.

"You'll make a bundle modeling," her cousin Yael had said as they'd suntanned on a Tel Aviv beach. "Then you can do anything you want."

"You could model *and* study," her best friend, Ronit, had added. "It's just posing. It can't be that time-consuming."

"And the army?" Shiva-Rose had reminded her friends of their mandatory military duty. "Are they going to wait while I'm on some runway in Milan?"

"For you they just might—think of how cute you'll look in fatigues!" her guy friend Rahm (on whom Shiva-Rose had had a lifelong crush) had teased.

So, fine, okay. She applied to appease them, but when the letter announcing her acceptance and offering her a full scholarship arrived, she got as caught up in the excitement as everyone else.

For her father, her acceptance to the summer program became something more, a sign almost. She should go, he'd told her. She should go and win. Like it would be a snap.

What went unsaid: She should spend July and August in another, relatively peaceful country. She'd be set for life, and he wouldn't have to worry about her.

Her own worries — about isolation, living among a bunch of superficial, giddy morons — got pushed aside. She was here; she was doing this. End of story.

"Attention, ladies! Attention! Our orientation is about to start."

Shiva-Rose glanced up and saw Victoria Devachan standing before them with a handheld microphone.

Time to get with the program, Shiva-Rose told herself. As the other girls took their seats, she checked out her rivals. As a group, they were a study in contrast — uniformity and diversity. Every possible complexion combination was represented, from translucent and pale to dark bittersweet chocolate. Every hair color on earth, and many mixed in chemical labs, every texture, length, and style was represented. Most girls wore sundresses, or tank tops, shorts, and flip-flops, and all sported name tags.

"Lindsay! Chloe! Over here!" called Alexis, who

seemed determined to have all four roommates be BFFs. Shiva-Rose, ever pragmatic, wanted to tell Alexis to not even bother.

Looking less than thrilled, Lindsay and Chloe made their way over to the group and sat in the chairs flanking Shiva-Rose and Alexis. Soon, all the other name tag–wearing girls had settled in, and Victoria began speaking again.

"How do you like our outdoor orientation spot?" she asked. "We chose this members-only club to give you a tiny taste of a model's life—*and* because an all-access pass to SoHo House is one of the prizes for the winner of our first challenge."

Shiva-Rose couldn't help feeling a trill of excitement, and the other girls shrieked and clapped.

"I'm getting ahead of myself," Ms. Devachan said, beaming. "We have much to cover, as you'll see on our monitor. Take a look at this rundown of our first session."

She gestured to the plasma screen. The photos of beautiful people had disappeared, and the display now read:

- Session One: July 1–July 15
- Competitors: 40

- Groups: Ten groups of four girls. Your group is comprised of your roommates.
- Competition: Photo shoot, July 15
- Ten Eliminations: Ten girls with the lowest combined scores will be asked to leave the program immediately.
- One Winner: The girl with the highest score for the photo shoot will be named the winner of the first session.

"As you can see, two weeks from today," Victoria said grandly, "we'll pick a winner for the first session of Top Model Prep. Starting Monday, you will spend every day in classes—two suites to a class—getting ready for the photo shoot challenge. You'll learn how to pose for a photographer and how to choose the right looks, among other important skills."

"Will we be graded?" a high-cheekboned Asian girl whose name tag read FAYE asked anxiously.

Victoria nodded. "Yes, after the photo challenge, grades ranging from A-plus to D-minus will be given out. Your final score will be an average of your solo shot grade and your grade in your group photo—the photo taken with your roommates. The girl with the combined highest score will win this challenge."

"But what if you rock the solo shot," asked a skinny girl with a high blond ponytail, whose name tag read—Shiva-Rose did a double take—BIKINI, "but get dragged down because of the group you're stuck in? I mean, that's so not fair."

Good point, Shiva-Rose thought, nibbling on her nail.

"I suggest you work with your team to take the best possible shot," Victoria answered evenly. "Teamwork is part of modeling. That's what you're here to learn."

Shiva-Rose distinctly heard Lindsay muffle her snort behind one hand.

"Please bring your attention to the next screen," Victoria was now saying. "It is my great pleasure to show you what the girl with the highest score from the photo challenge will win."

Prizes for the Winner of the Photo Shoot

- A $5000 Shopping Spree at Barneys!
- An all-access pass to a Spa Day at Soho House!
- An introduction in *Seventeen* magazine!
- Immunity for Session 2.

Appropriately, the model-hopefuls applauded wildly and shrieked again, each imagining herself with the windfall. Shiva-Rose gave their headmistress silent kudos for incentivizing her students. There wasn't a girl who now didn't want to win the first challenge.

Too bad only one of them could.

Shiva-Rose felt her heart beating faster, and her head whirled. Was she dizzy from being up this high, looking out over the sparkling spread of New York City? She'd never been scared of heights before, happily hiking to the top of Masada with friends to see the sunrise.

So was it just nerves?

To calm herself, Shiva-Rose did what she did best: She went into student mode. Fingers trembling, she unsnapped her beaten-up brown leather messenger bag and pulled out a pad of paper and a pen. As Victoria began speaking again, Shiva-Rose leaned forward and starting taking notes.

She was going to be a straight-A model.

Chapter Three
Boys on Billboards

"Thousands of high school students from all over the world applied to our program this summer," Victoria Devachan told her rapt audience, "and only forty were chosen. So give yourselves a hand for having made it this far."

Her audience erupted in a burst self-congratulatory applause. Lindsay did not clap. *She'd* made it this far for obvious reasons.

"Before we get to the nuts and bolts of our program, here are the most important things to remember: Top Model Prep is looking for the girl who embodies Modeling 2.0. She must be physically fit. We're done with the starved look, and good riddance to that!" Victoria pumped a wiry arm in the air.

Only a sprinkling of tentative applause greeted that one, Lindsay noted wryly. Even this crowd of know-nothings knew this much: The super-skinny model look was never going away. Half of these girls were naturally tall and slender. The other half? There were all sorts of ways to get skinny. In her Hollywood days, she'd seen too many girls—yeah, mostly white girls—abuse their bodies. Lindsay respected herself way too much for that. She'd done it right, by working out regularly to rid herself of any excess body fat. Which was not easy in her Staten Island neighborhood where the major food groups were Dunkin' Donuts, Domino's, and Dr. Pepper.

"A professional model is a girl who oozes confidence. If you're afraid, timid, or lack self-esteem, you won't last," Ms. Devachan told them.

Check, thought Lindsay, who had self-esteem in spades.

"The winner of Top Model Prep's summer program," Victoria continued, "will be a girl who's informed, who does her homework. At Top Model Prep, we're dedicated to breaking the stereotype of the model who's all beauty and no brains."

Suddenly Lindsay noticed that Shiva-Rose was taking *notes*. Lindsay felt like passing the girl a note of her own: *Forget the politically correct baloney Victoria spouts, you can't study to be a model. What you need to succeed won't be found in books or on Web sites, not even in these lessons.*

The bottom line was, you either had "it" or you didn't.

Shiva-Rose was not Lindsay's competition; she was too earthy, too out of step with American life (even if she was a fan of *Yes, We Blend*). And forget about freckle-faced pip-squeak Alexis. The girl wouldn't make it to the next session. In fact, Lindsay noticed no standouts among the forty hopefuls gathered on the roof. There was no doubt that the competition came down to her and Chloe Huntley, who Lindsay had seen giggling with "Aunt Vickie" the minute they'd set foot on the rooftop deck. The model-spawn was now hunched over her iPhone, speed texting.

Lindsay harrumphed. That girl would do anything to make herself appear busier, more important than anyone else. But Lindsay had to stamp out the little voice in her head that admitted: *Well, she kinda is.*

Victoria was now introducing Top Model Prep's official stylist, designer, and "visionary," Anabelle Trembley.

Anabelle wore owlish oversize sunglasses, a leopard-print blouse, and a long, colorful scarf (*a sure sign she's covering up loose neck skin*, Lindsay thought). While Victoria had exuded style, class, and canniness, the woman before them now zigzagged to a different beat. She spoke in breathy tones, punctuated with sweeping arm motions.

"Greetings, ladies!" Annabelle began. "I'm overjoyed to be here and hope to spend the summer enriching your lives. I will be one of your many professional instructors this summer, as well as a panelist and judge. Before we go into your schedule of classes, let this be your mantra: Our top model must show strength and character. Her beauty should radiate from inside. Be not just the fashion model, but the *role* model."

"Or get portrayed as one," Lindsay cracked to Alexis, who was sitting beside her and holding a huge knockoff Fendi bag. Lindsay wondered why Alexis would drag a giant tote to orientation—and why'd she'd even bothered to save her and Chloe seats. Lindsay would not have done the same.

Alexis popped a mini–hot dog into her mouth. "What do you mean, get portrayed as one?"

"The girl they pick will be told exactly what to do and say in public," Lindsay whispered. "She'll be exemplary, wear discreet hemlines, get good grades, and probably front that she's doing charity work. And she'd better not get caught doing un–role modely things like inappropriate drinking, dieting, or dating. That's how Top Model Prep rolls. Like Disney stars."

"You're so jaded!" Alexis said, and gently elbowed her.

"Real. It's called real. You'll see," Lindsay replied.

"It is now my distinct pleasure," Ms. Trembley cooed, "to present an overview of your classes and workshops. Specific, individual schedules have already been sent to your e-mail accounts."

With a flourish, she instructed the tech assistant to bring up the next screen.

The Modeling Arts

- Photo Shoots & Posing
- Runway Walking
- Fashion & Style
- Makeup Application
- Hairstyling
- Acting
- Go-Sees
- Personal Style
- Self-Esteem Workshops

As Ms. Trembley explained each class, Lindsay couldn't suppress a chuckle. How had such basics, in Trembley's clouded mind, been elevated to "Arts"? She wondered how Michelangelo would feel if he knew that walking and chest puffing were now in the same category with the Sistine Chapel.

"And now," Anabelle trilled, "I pass the baton to my brilliant colleague, Mr. Dan'yel Fieldstone, our chief makeup artist, genius creative director, and, as you'll see, guru of good. A beautiful soul." Anabelle pantomimed a worshipful pose as Top Model's next speaker took his place by the big screen.

"Please, don't get up." Dan'yel Fieldstone deadpanned. He had an unfortunate receding chin, chipmunk cheeks, and thinning hair. He adjusted his thick black-rimmed glasses and favored the group with an open smile.

"Victoria and Anabelle conspired and appointed me 'deliverer of the rules.' In other words, I get to play bad cop during this orientation." Hands on his hips, Tim Gunn–style, Dan'yel rolled his eyes toward the heavens. "I have no idea why they thought this would be a fitting role."

Snap judgment: Dan'yel was droll, self-deprecating, and very funny. And Lindsay was going to have trouble disliking him.

Dan'yel let out an exaggerated, put-upon sigh. "Roll the tape, gentlemen!"

With that, the screen filled with a new list.

The Rules

- No smoking
- No drugs
- No alcohol
- No cutting classes
- No accepting offers from agents or scouts outside of the program
- No overnight guests
- Participation in all challenges
- Obey curfew!—9 P.M. in your suite

"Most of these are self-explanatory," Dan'yel said. "But, that last one begs for interpretation. And frankly, ladies, the only interpretation is Top Model's."

"What do you think?" Alexis whispered to Lindsay. "They're really gonna enforce these rules, or are these just for show, too?"

Lindsay arched an eyebrow, wondering which one Alexis had already decided to break.

"The most important"—Dan'yel held a finger up for emphasis—"is our policy on going off campus—and by off campus, I mean, anywhere outside of our classrooms and housing. Your families have entrusted us with your safety, and we take that responsibility very seriously.

"So here's the deal. Whenever you need to leave the Top Model premises, you sign out, noting your destination, and then you sign back in. There's a sign-out sheet at the front desk in the Top Model Prep lobby that Victoria and I check every day. New York is a big city, and we need you to be alert and careful at all times. In the evenings, unless you're at a special function, you abide by a nine P.M. curfew. You will have charged cell phones on you at all times, and the front office phone number on speed dial."

"Do they give out LoJacks?" whispered a girl sitting behind Lindsay. She was a stunning, curvy Latina whose name tag read AVA.

"No, they surgically insert homing chips under your skin," giggled the girl next to her, a stick-thin brunette named Jana.

"I have to warn you, people, it's zero tolerance about that," Dan'yel continued. "Infraction of these rules leads to instant dismissal. So before you think about breaking any rules, think about this: Is it worth giving up your dream for?"

Silence greeted his warning, and then he broke into a grin. "I know, I had to end on a pithy note. Now, go relax and enjoy yourselves!" he said magnanimously. "Soak up the atmosphere of this very special place, and take some time to enjoy the city before classes start on Monday."

At those words, Alexis leaped up as if she'd been launched.

"Need a ladies' room break?" Shiva-Rose guessed.

"Need to get up and look around," Alexis answered, hoisting her bag over her shoulder. "This is my first time here and I want to see everything and take pictures. Come on!"

Lindsay wasn't particularly interested in playing pool-deck tourist, but she couldn't deny that Alexis's enthusiasm was infectious. When Shiva-Rose followed the small girl with the huge bag, Lindsay decided she might as well, too. It's not like there was anyone else she wanted to talk to.

Chloe, to Lindsay's chagrin, trailed along as well.

"That's got to be south," Alexis gestured. "I can see the Statue of Liberty!" She handed Shiva-Rose her camera, one of those cheap throwaways usually given away as party favors. "Take a picture of me with the statue in the background. Then I'll do you."

Shiva-Rose was happy to comply, but Lindsay noticed that the girl didn't seem to want one of her own taken. "We'll have plenty of posing to do soon enough," she said practically.

Then Alexis's attention was clearly captured by something else. She scooted over to the corner of the rooftop and pointed. Three words came out of her mouth: "Me. Want. That."

The others followed her gaze.

Alexis was looking . . . no, *staring,* at a billboard across the street. Granted, Lindsay allowed, the male model on it *was* a dreamboat: tanned and buff and gorgeous. But Alexis was acting as if the Greek god Adonis had stepped off Mount Olympus and fetchingly repositioned himself as an underwear model.

"Are those abs real, you think?" she asked breathlessly. "They look like someone chiseled them out of marble."

"I'm sure they're retouched," Chloe informed her, but Alexis shook her head emphatically, her eyes never leaving the billboard.

"He does have those come-hither eyes," Shiva-Rose offered.

"She's not looking at his eyes," Lindsay drawled.

"It's just, like . . . he's so . . . defined!" Alexis said in awe. "Is it even legal to have a billboard like this? Doesn't it cause accidents when drivers look up at it?"

"Welcome to New York," Lindsay said. She'd never been the boy-crazy type; most of the boys who'd been into her had only been interested in using her celeb status for their own personal gains. And she had a very specific type: tall, dark, and handsome. She rejected anyone who didn't fit within those confines.

"Well, he's not remotely as cute as my boyfriend back home," Chloe chimed in, and Lindsay's ears perked up. *Boyfriend?* That could be interesting.

"He's coming to visit next weekend," Chloe added proudly. "You'll see."

"There you are!" Dan'yel Fieldstone suddenly materialized by the girls, but he had eyes only for Chloe. "I just have to say it. You remind me so much of your mother."

Lindsay caught Chloe cringe. *Again, interesting.*

Turning to Lindsay, Shiva-Rose, and Alexis, Dan'yel said, "Chloe and I go back a long way. A hundred years ago, I was Charlotte's personal makeup artist. Anyway, darling, now that you're here, I was hoping to steal you away and introduce you to some people. Ken Paves, hairstylist to the stars, just so happens to be staying here at SoHo House with Anastasia Soare, *the* eyebrow guru. And, you have to meet Lorraine Schwartz, the jewelry designer—"

"Um," Chloe said, her fair cheeks turning pink. "Dan'yel, I don't mean to be ungrateful, but do we have to do this now? I'm not feeling all that great."

Lindsay didn't know whether to be shocked at Dan'yel's out-and-out favoritism, or awed by Chloe's sudden humility.

She settled on outraged.

Why don't Aunt Vickie and Dan'yel just crown the Pale Princess of the Pacific the winner and be done with it?

Not knowing what else to do, Lindsay spun on her heel and whipped out her cell phone. She had to call someone! But who? In her old life, she'd had an agent. A manager. She'd had *people.* They spoke up for her, protected her, made her life easier. She'd been stripped of her entire support system when she'd left Hollywood. Now, she had only her wits and cunning to rely on.

One thing about these last miserable years, she realized as she put her phone away, was that they'd toughened her up. All that time, she'd been laser-focused on getting back into the spotlight, being a star again. Now she had another goal.

Get Chloe Huntley eliminated.

Chapter Four
Death by Chocolate

It was *very* sensual.

As in, total immersion of all five senses, one more tantalizing than the next.

The aroma wafted onto the sidewalk from the restaurant in Union Square, Alexis's instant favorite New York neighborhood. The smells, more intense inside, were dizzying, intoxicating. Like breathing pure cocoa laced with sugarcane.

Then came the colors, a soothing palate of cocoas, deep rich browns, savory caramels, burnt oranges, and ivory creams. Everywhere you turned, shelves were piled high with boxes of bonbon assortments, tins, and jars of brightly wrapped gifts. The phrase *eye candy* had been invented for this place.

Touching was tempting. The crunchy waffle balls were unwrapped, piled high, waiting to be rolled between thumb and forefinger. The barrel of swirling molten-thick liquid begged for dipping fingers.

The sounds were a sweet symphony of pure pleasure. Of laughter, squeals, and excitement, murmurs of rapture.

In the end, it was the taste. That's what sealed the deal. The deep, rich flavors. Ultimate bliss.

Alexis Cournos had found paradise.

She was so glad that she'd convinced her roommates to come explore with her. It was Saturday night, classes didn't start until Monday, and she'd wanted nothing more than to experience New York City. It had taken some cajoling, though.

"Chocolate?" Lindsay had made her repeat it as they got ready in their suite. "You want us to go to a candy store?"

"It's an *experience*," Alexis, who'd read about the place in her guidebook, promised. "Not a store."

"Max Brenner? Some new designer? I never heard of him," Chloe sniffed as she applied her Smashbox lip gloss.

"It's Max Brenner, the bald man," Alexis tried to explain. "He designs—"

"Technically," Shiva-Rose cut in, brushing out her long, thick hair, "it's Max Brenner, Chocolate by the Bald Man. It's a theme restaurant that was started by two Israelis, Max Fichtman and Oded Brenner. They have Chocolate by the Bald Man shops all over Israel, Australia, the Philippines, and two here in New York."

"Then you *gotta* come, Shiva-Rose — represent for the homeland!" Alexis punctuated her statement with a fist in the air.

"Ix-nay on the urban-speak, sista," Lindsay snapped. "You're white and from the Midwest."

"Isn't your boyfriend coming next weekend?" Alexis ignored Lindsay and turned to Chloe, who nodded, her face lighting up. "They have a gift shop. You could surprise him with a chocolate heart or something," Alexis coaxed.

"Or those extra pounds you'll want to put on, just for him?" Lindsay clearly couldn't help herself.

An hour later, four models-to-be were seated at a primo table on the upper tier of the restaurant. It was a vantage point from which they could see, and more important, be seen. Alexis hadn't considered the impact they might make, the four of them in public together. There was platinum-haired classic Chloe, olive-skinned stunner Shiva-Rose,

African-American beauty Lindsay, and herself, representing, she guessed, the redheaded, freckled type.

Their entrance had not gone without notice. Heads had turned. Eyes had followed them. She could practically hear the whispers and see the thought bubbles over the customers' heads: *Are they celebrities? The cast of* Gossip Girl*? They must be famous.*

Now her roommates studied their menus, pretending not to notice all the attention they were getting. Maybe *they* were used to the stares, the gawking. But this was a first for Alexis.

"I can't eat anything here. It's all a bazillion calories." Lindsay snapped the menu closed.

"There's salad," Shiva-Rose pointed out helpfully.

"No one eats salad here," declared Alexis, "it's against the law."

Well, if it wasn't, it should've been. The menu was a spiral-bound booklet of chocolate heaven, a cornucopia of everything you could dream of, and lots you couldn't. Like chocolate fondue, chocolate waffles, chocolate pizza, molten-chocolate heart cake.

"How are you ladies today?" A cute curly-haired blond waiter in a tight black T-shirt—too bad it was under a chocolate-colored apron—greeted them. Alexis blushed.

"Can I get you something to drink first?" Another identically attired waiter, this one green-eyed and olive-skinned, was on his heels.

As Lindsay and Chloe were explaining the exact brand of bottled water they required, a third hottie showed up. "Do you have any questions about anything on the menu?" he asked. This one was a total Tyson Beckford doppelgänger. Alexis's heart quickened.

"What do you recommend?" she asked him, batting her lashes. She was flirting outrageously, but at least she didn't blurt: *Yes, I have a question: Are you on the menu?*

"The chocolate chunks are especially yummy," curly-boy said helpfully.

"That's what I'll be if I eat them, a chocolate chunk," Lindsay grumbled.

"Since there are four of you, why not share the Chocolate Mess?" Tyson (Alexis named him) suggested. "You eat it right out of the pan with a spatula, there's mountains of ice cream and cake and whipped cream—"

Cool!

Lindsay elbowed her sharply. So, probably, no.

"Here's what a lot of people do." The green-eyed one saw his opening. "Close your eyes, then open the menu to any random page. Put your finger down—whatever it falls on, you order. You can't go wrong here. Everything's off the charts."

"Excellent!" This time, Alexis's enthusiasm won over her risk-averse roommates.

Blind ordering was a blast, and they ended up with everything from ice cream, to fondue with fruit and brownies, and s'mores, too.

When the trio of waiters left, Chloe turned to Alexis, her blue eyes teasing. "You drooled over billboard-boy, and you could barely keep from kissing that one waiter. Have you never been up close and personal with a cute guy before?"

Alexis felt herself blushing again. She couldn't bear to admit to the girls that she'd never had a boyfriend.

"Well, no one could approach *your* level of experience," Lindsay taunted Chloe.

“At least I’m *in* a relationship,” Chloe retorted crisply. “Unlike you, I assume?”

“Please.” Lindsay waved the insult away without answering Chloe’s question. “All guys want to date models. It’s so superficial.”

Shiva-Rose folded her arms and rolled her eyes at the exchange.

She’s so serious, Alexis thought. *Like a scientist.*

When their treats arrived, Shiva-Rose spoke again, confirming Alexis’s opinion of her.

“Did you know that smelling is more stimulating than eating, because there are more sensory receptors in your nose than in your mouth?” Shiva-Rose asked, taking a dainty bite of a s’more. “It’s true.”

“Check it out, eleven o’clock.” Chloe suddenly brought their attention to an older guy with a neatly trimmed salt-and-pepper beard who was heading toward them.

“Excuse me,” he said, “I don’t mean to intrude, but I couldn’t help noticing. Are you gals models?”

“It so happens we are,” Lindsay instantly turned on the charm.

"No, we're not," Chloe contradicted.

"Not yet," Alexis clarified.

"I see there's some difference of opinion," he said with a laugh. He reached inside his suit jacket and extracted a business card, "Just in case, I run a boutique talent agency. Are you looking for representation?"

"What agency—" Lindsay started, but Chloe wasn't having it.

"No, we're not. Thank you anyway."

"What's wrong with you?" Lindsay stared Chloe down as the agent, leaving his card on the table, backed away.

"I'm not talking to some random stranger—"

"It could be an opportunity—"

"Chloe's right," Shiva-Rose put in, "It's against the rules to talk to agents."

Just then a gaggle of tween girls at the next table pointed cameras at them. "Oh, sorry, I'm not doing pictures," Lindsay told them.

"Of course we will," said Chloe, getting to her feet. "They want *us* to take *their* picture. Get over yourself."

Doubly annoyed, Lindsay turned on Alexis. "Why did you drag us here?"

"It's a trap," Chloe whispered. "Willy Wonka's gonna come out and stuff you with a bazillion calories. Stop being so paranoid, Lindsay. How much damage can Alexis do?"

Hmmmm, thought Alexis. There were certain people back in Hamtramck who could give her a real answer to that. But it's not like anyone had ever been permanently damaged by Alexis's impulsiveness.

"It's pretty simple," Alexis said breezily as she dipped a strawberry into the chocolate fondue. "I thought it'd be cool to get to know each other in a casual, fun place where not everyone is running around trying to out-beautiful everyone else."

"But we *are* competitors, not friends," Shiva-Rose reminded them.

"Can't we be both?" Alexis asked, feeling a pang of disappointment.

"No." Chloe and Lindsay said it at the same time, Chloe with regret, Lindsay with force. "Look, things move quickly here," Lindsay went on. "We can be as friendly as we want now, but when we start getting judged and scored, you'll see what I mean. There are forty of us, and only one can win. As people start getting eliminated, you'll see how fast friendship takes a dive out the window."

"I hate to agree with her, but inevitably it will get unpleasant. I've seen it." Chloe said. Just then her phone made a chirping sound. An incoming text. Judging by the way her pale eyes lit up, it was obviously her LA BF.

"Is that your boyfriend texting you? What's his name?" Alexis asked.

"Liam," Chloe breathed, as if the name were holy. "Liam Lattimore. He's the son of the California senator, James Lattimore."

Out of the corner of her eye, Alexis caught Lindsay making a gagging motion at Shiva-Rose, who hid her smile. Alexis wondered why Lindsay was so bitter; she thought it was amazing that Chloe had found true love, especially with a rich Prince Charming.

"Can I ask you a question, Lindsay?" Alexis said, truly curious.

"Go for it."

"You've already made it as actress. Why would you even want to model?"

"Isn't it usually the other way around, models trying to be actresses?" Shiva-Rose sounded as if she, too, had been wondering about that.

"This is her comeback," Chloe said, looking up from her iPhone and spooning butterscotch ice cream into her mouth.

"It's not a comeback." Lindsay stopped her coldly. "It's a reinvention."

Chloe rolled her eyes. Instantly, Alexis got it. Lindsay probably *had* been trying, in vain, to get back into acting. Modeling was another route to the spotlight. And Lindsay really cared about being famous.

"What's so great about being a star?" The question slipped out before Alexis even realized it.

"Are you kidding?" Lindsay's cheeks were aglow and her eyes danced as she began describing the lifestyle she coveted. "It's amazing! You're treated like royalty. Everyone's doing things for you—before you even ask! And giving you free stuff. That knockoff Fendi you've been toting around?" She pointed to Alexis's designer satchel, and for a second Alexis panicked. Did Lindsay somehow know that she'd picked it up when the street vendor had looked the other way?

"When she's a successful model, she'll be able to buy the real thing?" Shiva-Rose guessed.

"Even better," Lindsay said. "When you're a successful model, actor, star, whatever, you never have to *buy* anything. You get expensive stuff for free. Seriously, don't any of you read *Us Weekly*? Fendi just sponsored Dita Von Teese's birthday party—in Paris!"

"What's a Dita Von Teese?" Alexis asked, relieved that no one realized she hadn't bought the bag. Of course, she'd been unaware that it was a fake. She wouldn't be so naïve next time.

"What does *sponsored* mean, they paid for the party?" Shiva-Rose asked.

"Paid for it?" Lindsay practically sputtered. "They chartered a private jet, and flew her and, oh, hundreds of other stars, to Paris, where they rented out a nightclub, hired professional DJs, catered the whole thing. And, she got a free bag. Obviously."

"What did the lovely Ms. Von Teese have to do in return?" Chloe's attention had been piqued.

"Pose for a few pictures, that's all." Lindsay shrugged. "What's your point, Chloe? You, of all people, know the game."

"A few pictures, huh? I'll bet you anything Fendi made sure there were more photographers than guests at the party," Chloe said with distaste.

"Again. Your point?" Lindsay was clearly irritated at being interrupted.

"They don't do it out of the goodness of their hearts, or because she's so talented or revered. It's publicity. It's the same thing when they give you a free iPhone"—Chloe held hers in the air—"or jewelry or clothes. They want to be sure the world sees their products on the pages of magazines."

"That doesn't take away from the fabulous freebie-ness of it all," Lindsay responded. "They can't take back the party. You get an amazing night, meeting stars, dancing—having the time of your life. So what if a picture of you, looking fabulous, ends up in *People*. Where's the downside?"

Alexis nodded, silently siding with Lindsay. She shot a glance at Shiva-Rose, who was looking contemplative.

"Ask Britney. Or LiLo. Or anyone caught in a compromising position," Chloe reminded her.

"That won't happen to me," swore Lindsay.

Chloe said, "These companies just use celebrities, models, athletes, whatever, as props. The minute the next younger, cuter girl comes along, you're over. I'd think *you*, of all people, would get that."

Harsh, Alexis thought.

"Me? Are you saying my career took a dive because someone newer came along?"

"You haven't had much of a career lately," Chloe pointed out.

Lindsay's jaw tightened. "That was an entirely different situation. I could have done features after *Yes, We Blend* was canceled. There were scripts piled up at my door. Everyone wanted me. But I was thirteen years old, and I don't exactly have supportive stage parents. They hauled me back to Staten Island. But my real home is Hollywood, baby. And once I'm back, it'll be for good." Lindsay lifted her chin.

Alexis listened, shocked at the exchange. Chloe had really zinged Lindsay—called her a has-been to her face! But Lindsay neither looked nor sounded wounded. An act? If so, then Lindsay Robinson was one heck of an actress.

Almost as good as Alexis Cournos.

Abruptly, Alexis picked up the big bag—fake or not, it'd do the trick—and excused herself to go to the bathroom. Only she didn't go directly there. Instead, she sashayed to the front of the restaurant, the chocolate-themed gift shop.

While examining the gift set of cocoa body butter, and then the stacked fondue sets, she made sure her back was to the security camera. When no one was looking, she rearranged the shelves to cover up the empty spaces she'd created.

She meandered around the restaurant, threading her way among the tables. The place was packed. One cute couple was feeding each other like they were practicing for a wedding cake picture. Bunches of bubbly tourists crowded around too-small tables. Alexis kept walking until she found what she was looking for: An entire group had gotten up to pose for a picture, leaving a credit card unattended on the table.

"It's on me," she told her roommates later on when the bill came.

Chapter Five
Like Mother . . .

"Welcome to your first day of classes, models!"

Bright and early Monday morning, creative director Dan'yel greeted the summer students as they filed in to Top Model Prep's photo studio. Most were yawning, still half asleep and clutching Starbucks Venti skim lattes.

Except for Chloe.

Chloe had gotten a solid eight hours of sleep, fully expecting to be up-and-at-'em early. She knew better than anyone that professional models led glamorous lives only when they weren't working. For classes, for shoots, for go-sees and other assignments, tardy was not an option. Modeling was actually . . . work. A job.

According to the schedules they'd been e-mailed, all students were expected to attend between two and four classes per day, with an hour for lunch. All classes would be held in the

Top Model building in the various studios, lofts, and spaces belonging to the school.

The girls of 14C were sharing every class with the girls of 14A, who lived across the hall—Faye, Jana, Bikini, and Ava. Today their first class was photography taught by Dan'yel and, Chloe assumed, some up-and-coming photographer hoping to make his mark by shooting students, perhaps even discovering a hot new talent. The shutterbug had not made an entrance yet, so far as she could tell.

Chloe checked out her surroundings. The loft space was identical to so many others she'd hung out in waiting for her mom to be photographed, finished, and ready to take her home. Top Model's photo studio was cluttered with tripods, cameras, lighting setups, light-bouncing umbrellas—even amplifiers and CD players scattered about. Eye-catching blowups of framed magazine covers dotted the walls.

"These amazing covers aren't just here because they're works of art," Dan'yel said dramatically as he drew the group's attention to the posters. "Each one was photographed right here, in this studio."

"No way!" Jana shook her head, pointing to a

recent cover of *Vogue*. "This model is standing in a forest."

"The magic of photography!" Alexis piped up.

"It's done with special effects," said Faye.

"Like, with computers?" the unfortunately named Bikini offered.

"I hope it's not a green screen," whined Ava. "Green is so not my color."

"Only redheads can do green," agreed Bikini.

See, this is why models are stereotyped as dummies, Chloe thought, catching Shiva-Rose rolling her eyes at the absurdity.

"Look up." Dan'yel directed them to a giant roller hung just inches from the ceiling. He nodded to an assistant, who was holding a remote control. At her touch, the roller unspooled a huge sheet of patterned fabric that fell all the way to the floor. Presto! The background was now a copse of trees. Another fabric background was a realistic-looking street scene; yet another was a grand circular staircase. Some were monochromatic, for close-ups.

"Is that a real wind machine?" asked Alexis, tossing her hair over her shoulder. "So we can look wind-blown?"

"It's a fan," Dan'yel said. "And we have water hoses, too, in case a model needs to have that 'caught in the rain' look."

Several of the girls instinctively reached to pat their hair down.

"Don't worry, we won't soak you in the first session. We're saving that until later," Dan'yel reassured them.

Dan'yel pointed to a vintage cover of *Seventeen* magazine. "If we're going for natural light instead of a specific background, we make use of our loft's enormous windows. The best time of day to shoot is late afternoon, when the sun is waning. That gives us the best light. He paused expectantly. "So, who recognizes the model here?"

A fresh-faced blond wearing a pink sundress graced the cover. Her expression — bow lips pursed, blue eyes focused off in the distance — made her seem chic, but curious. Wide-eyed, innocent, and pretty, the quintessential preppy model of her day was as recognizable as the president of the US.

Every single person in the room turned to stare. A few girls actually gasped. And Chloe Huntley, dead ringer for her mother, wished she could fall through the floor and disappear.

Why were they doing this to her?

Victoria was bad, but Dan'yel was the worst, a repeat offender. Wasn't it enough for them that she was *here*? Wasn't it enough that she now summoned her default smile she was so well trained in, the "on command" dazzling display of her perfect white veneers, no matter how she really felt inside? Veneer, it struck her, was a very good word.

"That's Charlotte Huntley," Shiva-Rose reported, loud and clear, like the good student she was.

"She's your *mother*?" Alexis, ever the naïf, said it out loud as she whirled on Chloe. "Why didn't you say so?"

"Pu-leeze, she made it clear from day one," Lindsay grumbled.

Still fake-beaming, Chloe hoped her eyes sent Dan'yel a different signal. It must have worked, as he finally continued.

"Of course, what makes a great portrait, or piece of modeling art, isn't the environment, or even the model herself. The lighting, these backgrounds, even the makeup, hairstyles, and fashions themselves are merely tools in a real model's box of tricks. That trick, which we hope to teach you, is to make each photo an expression of you."

To: Liam From: Chloe

Veneer. The coat of armor they force
me to wear.
Underneath, I sneer. Underneath, I fear
It will ever be thus.

Send

She sent her poem to Liam.

When she looked up from her screen, she raised her hand and excused herself. Chloe suddenly felt the need to express herself to someone else.

"What a lovely surprise," Victoria purred as Chloe showed up unannounced at her lavish top floor office. "But you caught me multitasking." She gestured apologetically from the iced Venti latte and cup of fruit salad on her desk to the fanned-out photos of models and fashion magazines.

Chloe stood awkwardly in the doorway as Victoria removed the Bluetooth device from her ear and motioned for her to come in. "The first week of a new session is always crazy!"

A moment ago, it had seemed urgent to confront Victoria. Now, Chloe wasn't so sure. Maybe she ought to have waited a bit, at least compose her thoughts. She didn't want to come off bratty.

The headmistresses sat behind a sleek glass-and-chrome desk. Everything about Victoria's office was couture correct, fashionably perfect for her position as Top Model Prep's headmistress, from the framed original signed sketches of designer dresses on the walls to the gracefully arched windows and soft, flattering lighting.

"Sorry for barging in," Chloe began, but Victoria cut her off.

"Barge in? You? Don't be silly. But you should have called. I could have made a lunch reservation at Momofuku. *The* most impossible-to-get table, but I can pull a few strings in this town."

"See, that's exactly what I wanted to talk about," Chloe said, regaining some of her resolve.

"Lunch?" Victoria consulted her watch, a Patek Philippe. "It's not too late for a lunch reservation. I can still call David Chang, he's the owner, and a great friend."

Chloe perched on the edge of the chair, leaning forward. "I'm not making myself clear. I don't want special treatment."

"I'm not sure I understand, honey. Special, how?" The woman pinned Chloe with her inquisitive brown eyes and warm smile.

Was Victoria being purposely dense? "I mean, would you ask one of the other students out to lunch?"

"None of the other students is the daughter of an old friend." Victoria still seemed not to get what Chloe was saying.

"It's just — you and well, it's more Dan'yel — keep saying that in front of all the other girls. Singling me out. For being Charlotte Huntley's daughter."

"You say it like it's a bad thing!" Victoria's eyebrows, expertly tinted to match her hair color, arched a tad. "There are worse reasons to be singled out. Unless . . . is there something I don't know? Are you and Charlotte having a tiff?"

"No," Chloe mumbled.

"Charlotte and I came up together in the modeling world, as you know. We remained great friends."

Translation: Charlotte is a big contributor to Top Model Prep. This year, she contributed her daughter. And BTW, if she were here, she would remind you that you didn't exactly "come up together." She's ten years younger than you are, Aunt Vickie.

"She only wants the best for you," Victoria said. "She wants you to be happy. So do we."

"I'd actually prefer if my mother wasn't referenced again." There, Chloe had said it. "I hope you understand."

"Are you concerned about high expectations? Is that it, honey? It's understandable. But you shouldn't worry about being in Charlotte's shadow. You'll make your own name for yourself."

"No, no, it's not that," Chloe said. How could she tell this woman, a former supermodel who embraced this world so much she ran a school, that Charlotte's model-shadow only meant something to other people, not to her? She was flustered, but determined to get her point across. "It's just, well, it's only been a couple of days, but Dan'yel practically pulled me away from the other girls at orientation, and today at photo class, he—"

"Oh, so it's the other girls. Are they giving you a hard time because they think you have an advantage over them? Girls can be very cruel to each other, and if there's a problem I want to know about it."

"Do I have an advantage, Ms. Devachan?" Chloe pronounced it formally.

"Look in the mirror, dear."

"Everyone who got into this program is beautiful. They're all model-worthy." Chloe reminded her.

"But everyone here does not have your poise, your background, the kind of education you can't buy. Everyone here is not part of a modeling dynasty."

Chloe grimaced. If there was a word she hated more than *model* it was *dynasty*. It reminded her of *destiny,* a future you didn't get to choose.

Victoria pushed back on her chair. The wheels rolled lightly on the polished bamboo floor. "If you feel you're being singled out for standing out, even among all these beautiful girls, my advice is to enjoy it. Life is easier for beautiful people, Chloe. I don't have to tell you that. Of course it's unfair, but it's true. Human beings are hardwired to appreciate beauty. As a beautiful young woman, you will be treated better, cut the line, as it were, everywhere. And if I were you, I wouldn't fight it. Because it won't last forever."

"I don't want—"

"What? To win unfairly? Is that what you're saying?" Victoria narrowed her eyes, looking suddenly taken aback.

Chloe flashed back to the most recent argument she'd had with her mother before leaving for the airport. "If I win," Chloe had cried, "everyone's going to say it's because I'm your daughter."

"That's the beauty of it," Charlotte had said. "Victoria Devachan made her reputation on her scrupulous honesty. If you ask me, that's what ended her career. She'll be so thrilled to have you, she'll fawn all over you and treat you like a VIP. But don't confuse that with cheating. Victoria would never, ever allow it. You'll win because there's no one who comes close to you. You were born to be a supermodel. But you need to get started now. You're sixteen. It's late."

Now, standing in New York, Chloe shook her head. "I didn't mean that at all, Victoria."

Victoria Devachan went on to practically parrot Charlotte Huntley, almost as if they'd planned this summer, conspired together. "If it makes you feel any better," she said, "I'll let you in on a little secret. Top Model Prep has a sterling reputation, and I would never sully it. No matter what you may think, no matter who is praising you, singling you out, this competition is not fixed. If you win, it will be because you've earned it. Trust me on that."

It was that simple then.

Chloe had to figure out a way to not earn it.

Chapter Six
The Photographer

Shiva-Rose felt bad for Chloe, who had obviously left the photo class because of the whole my-mother-is-famous fiasco. But Shiva-Rose was enjoying herself immensely; so far, photography was like history and science class wrapped up in one luxe package. She cupped her chin in her hand and listened to Dan'yel talk.

"The photographs on our walls were taken by legendary fashion photographers like Herb Ritts, Annie Leibovitz, and David LaChappelle," he was saying. "Today, I have the pleasure of introducing you to our own legend in the making. He'll be photographing you and teaching you about expressions and how to get that one best shot. He's a young man on the brink, tomorrow's superstar photographer. Mack Scarborough, come up and let's get to work!"

Dan'yel gestured to a guy no one had noticed standing in the shadows. *How long has he been leaning languidly against that back wall?* Shiva-Rose wondered, her pulse picking up.

The class swiveled around in their seats to see—and their reaction was instantaneous. Some girls tittered. Some waved or winked seductively. One whistled. Alexis whispered to Shiva-Rose, "He should be the model! He's got more going on, then, well, that dude on the billboard!"

And Shiva-Rose couldn't help but agree.

Mack propelled himself off the wall and headed to the front of the room. A white tank exposed muscled shoulders, wide enough to hold multiple camera straps. His dark brown hair was slicked back, tucked behind his ears, and just long enough to tickle the back of his ropy neck. One unruly shock of hair fell fetchingly over his forehead. As his piercing green eyes swept the room, his full lips formed a natural smirk. He wore jeans and battered brown boots.

Mack didn't feign embarrassment at the girls' gazes. Did that make him a practical guy who was used to being stared at?

Or just an egocentric jerk?

They'd know soon enough, Shiva-Rose determined. But the guy sure did know how to make an impression.

"The photographer has a lot of power in a model's life," Dan'yel told the girls. "Many people believe he can make or break careers. If he doesn't connect with the model, her photo can be dismal. On the other hand, if there is a connection, if he sees something in you . . ."

It was in that moment that Mack glanced at Shiva-Rose. The look was fleeting, but it said, "I see *you*." Shiva-Rose felt a flush pass through her. She hoped no one else noticed.

"A model's purpose when photographed is usually to sell something—an outfit, a designer, a magazine, a car, anything you're hired for."

Without preamble, the photographer had addressed the class. Mack Scarborough had the kind raspy boy voice Shiva-Rose had a weakness for. She thought of her back-home crush, Rahm, and realized how young and immature he seemed in comparison to Mack.

"Today"—Mack gazed meaningfully around the room—"you're going to sell *me* . . ." He paused in a way that made a few of the girls squirm.

"Sell you what?" asked an obviously smitten Bikini.

"On who you are, on what you're saying," Mack replied. "For the first shot, we'll keep it simple. I'm going to assign each of you a flower. Through your expression, you'll interpret the *essence* of that flower—convince me, and my camera, that you *are* flora."

"Who's Flora?" Jana asked nervously.

Shiva-Rose broke out laughing. She was one of the few who did, and she caught Mack give her a quick, dazzling smile.

"So where are the flowers?" Bikini scoured the room.

"Inside each one of you," Mack said, offering a satisfied smirk.

Which confused at least half the girls.

Dan'yel stepped in to edify. "There are no actual flowers, and you're going to be doing these shots in the clothes you have on now."

Whining, pouting, and groans reverberated around the room. "No way! Unfair! Why'd I wear this . . . ? I have to go change!" In the midst of the chaos, Shiva-Rose spied Chloe slipping back into the classroom, looking a bit flustered. She took her seat and checked her iPhone.

"What you're wearing is irrelevant," Mack explained. "This is an exercise in posing, in choosing how to use your face and body to express what you are. It's about imagination."

Had he winked at her? Or had Shiva-Rose inexplicably hallucinated?

"I think he's already made his choice," Lindsay whispered, nudging Shiva-Rose.

"You're deluded." Shiva-Rose sounded surer of herself than she felt.

"Oh, like you didn't notice?" Alexis challenged.

"Notice what?" Shiva-Rose said.

Lindsay smirked. "Here's some free advice. If a straight male photographer who can help you win this competition is flirting — which he totally is — use him. This isn't high school. It doesn't matter if you *like* him."

Shiva-Rose bristled. Mostly because Lindsay was making sense and she *didn't* like it one bit. *And besides*, she told herself as she watched Mack begin working with the other group, *Lindsay could be wrong. Mack knows he's hot. He probably flirts with lots of girls.*

"Fine, go ahead and lose. Better odds for me." Lindsay gave a self-satisfied shrug.

Once the photographer had given the first group their assignments, he strode over to them. He had swagger. Shiva-Rose liked swagger in a guy—as long as he could back it up with real strength of character.

"So who's who in this group?" he asked, getting right to the point. Up close, he was even more handsome. As the girls introduced themselves, Shiva-Rose wondered how old he was. Probably you had to be at least in your midtwenties to teach a course, no?

Mack made a show of squinting, framing them with his hands, sizing them up behind the camera lens.

"I'm going to pose you as a bunch," he decided, stroking his scruffy chin. "We'll start with solo shots, then all together in a bouquet. Alexis," he said, "I see you as a wildflower. Think about it; what will your interpretation be? How will you express it?"

There was a glimmer of mischief in Alexis's eye. It was clear that posing as a wildflower appealed to her.

"Chloe, you'll be a daisy."

If picture-perfect Chloe was offended at being perceived as such a common flower, she didn't show it.

Lindsay, unsurprisingly, chaffed at his choice for her. "A black-eyed Susan? *Really?* Isn't that a little . . . oh, I don't know . . . ghetto?"

Truly taken aback, Mack looked flustered. Which — Shiva-Rose hated to admit it — made him even cuter.

"You know, a daisy but with a *black* center?" she taunted him. "I see myself more as a rose. Unless you were saving that for *Shiva*-Rose?"

Shiva-Rose's back went up, feeling as if Lindsay had dissed her.

"You completely misinterpret," Mack said in a bid to retrieve the upper hand. "But if it's so important for you to be a rose for the class exercise, go for it." Lindsay nodded triumphantly.

"As for you — " Mack's voice turned even raspier — or was she imagining it? — as he turned to her. " — Shiva-Rose." She nodded, her skin tingling. "Are you Israeli?" he guessed, and she nodded once again. A smile tugged at Mack's full lips. "I see delicacy laced with strength, a girl who doesn't give up her secrets willingly. . . ."

All her life, Shiva-Rose'd been taught to look people in the eye. So why, under Mack's scrutiny, did she lower her gaze? Worse, Shiva-Rose found herself blushing, fidgeting, tugging her long sleeves over her knuckles, grasping the fabric in her fingers.

"Shiva-Rose, I dub you calla lily."

As Mack set up his photo equipment and the girls chatted, Shiva-Rose found her imagination stunted. She could not think of how to embody a calla lily, and told her roomies as much.

Chloe, unexpectedly, came to her rescue. "Here," she said, handing Shiva-Rose her iPhone. "I Googled *calla lily*. Looking at a picture and reading the description might help."

"Thank you!" Shiva-Rose exclaimed. She wouldn't forget Chloe's generosity. "Do you know what your interpretation is going to be?" Shiva-Rose asked Alexis, who nodded, grinning.

"A wildflower," declared Alexis imperiously, "follows no rules."

Alexis wasn't a big fan of rules. That became obvious to everyone watching as she posed for her solo shots. Rarely did she take Mack's directions. If he said, "Shift your weight between your hips," she twirled on her toe, laughing unself-consciously. She ran her hands through her hair, tossed it about, then faced the camera with a sly wink.

Shiva-Rose did not think Mack, nor Dan'yel, would appreciate Alexis's stubborn independence in the first photo class.

Instead, it worked for her.

"Brilliant!" Mack said, clicking away all the while.

Jana and Bikini were up next, doing, respectively, daffodils and peonies. Mack proved to be chameleonlike with his direction, adjusting his style to his models' abilities. Which, in this case, translated to kindergarten teacherspeak instead of the no-nonsense photographer he'd appeared to be. He coddled Jana and Bikini, gushing over them. And never used a word of more than two syllables.

Shiva-Rose wasn't the only one to notice it.

"Note how he condescends," Lindsay commented. "I bet he's had a lot of experience shooting models."

"I think that probably makes him good at his job." The words were out of Shiva-Rose's mouth before she could stop them.

"Yeah, you would think that."

"Lindsay Robinson," Dan'yel called, "you're up."

Lindsay, ever the actress, mimed various roses. A bratty pout, arms akimbo, really impressed Dan'yel. "Look at you, Miss Thorny Rose! Ouch, prickly, aren't you?" Lindsay stretched upward, as petals might, tilted her head toward an imaginary sun. Then she curled up into a ball, and Mack cheered, "Rosebud. Good job!"

Hmmm. Shiva-Rose wondered if Mack really did like what he saw through his lens, or if he was just, in different ways, being encouraging to everyone?

She got her answer soon enough. One of the girls from 14A, Faye, did an interpretation of a sunflower that Mack was not happy with. "You're obviously a smart cookie, Faye, but this interpretation—you look like a soldier, marching off to war. It's way off base and does you no justice."

Faye tried to explain that sunflowers were strong, independent, thriving plants, and that's what she was trying to show.

"Yes, but they're not robots. A model needs to bring out the essence of a sunflower, not pantomime a report. You overthought it. Go back and try again."

Shiva-Rose felt a stab of pity for the girl, who hung her shiny dark head. She felt the tiniest twinge of nervousness, too, wondering if Mack would be just as hard on her.

Chloe went next—the daisy. She pulled her hair in a tight ponytail atop her head and posed with her jaw resting on her fists. Her lips were parted slightly, in neither a smile nor frown, and she looked straight at the camera, eyebrows up slightly to form a quizzical look. *Boring*, Shiva-Rose thought.

But Mack was glowingly complimentary to every single pose. *Is he laying it on thick just because it's Chloe?* Shiva-Rose wondered.

"Shiva-Rose?" Mack turned to her. "Let's see how my calla lily looks behind the lens."

Okay. Go-time. She would not come unhinged, not freeze, and definitely not overdo it. *Focus. Focus.* Shiva-Rose took a deep breath, smiled politely, and began the poses she'd imagined after looking at the picture of the flower.

She'd only done one pose—hugging her knees, looking down—before the photographer stopped to praise her.

"That's it. Do that again! Okay, now turn away from the sun — beautiful!"

More pleased with herself than she wanted to admit, Shiva-Rose exhaled. "Perfect!" Mack announced. "Now let's see those downcast eyes, shy . . . now inward . . . now searching, mysterious. Yes. You are the soul of the calla lily."

Shiva-Rose felt like he was seeing right through her. And she sort of liked it.

Finally, it was time to get their evaluations.

"We're going over your photos for two reasons," Dan'yel reminded them. "To prepare you for the big photo challenge ahead, but more important, to teach you. By examining your best shots, you'll get constructive criticism, see what you might've done differently, and hear positive reinforcement, for those of you who got it right the first time out."

That turned out to be one person only — Chloe.

"I gave you the simplest, some would say, most commonplace flower. But you made it your own," Mack gave her props.

Really? It suddenly struck Shiva-Rose that Chloe's expression mimicked the one Charlotte

Huntley had done for that *Seventeen* cover decades prior. Personally, she didn't think either was that special, but Mack explained, projecting a shot of Chloe, face forward, fingers laced under her chin, lips forming a Mona Lisa mystery-smile.

"This is the perfect shot. You're centered, still, but your eyes are asking, 'He loves me? He loves me not. . . .' It's profound!"

Which is when Shiva-Rose saw the brilliance in Chloe's seemingly simple interpretation.

And when Lindsay wilted.

Chapter Seven
Hatching a Plan

Chloe was a sound sleeper. That was a stroke of luck. Lindsay had totally figured the model-heiress would go to bed with Bliss moisturizer slathered on her face and a silk mask over her eyes. Beauty sleep didn't come cheaply. But the sweet rhythmic snoring, the sign of deep sleep, was just an added bonus.

Bonus round two: Chloe slept on her side, knees drawn to her chest, facing away from her night table. Where her iPhone was.

Lindsay lingered a microsecond before liberating the pricey cell phone from its charger. In repose, Chloe seemed so innocent, almost fragile. *Doesn't matter*, Lindsay reminded herself as she backed silently out of Chloe's darkened bedroom. The competition was rigged, Chloe was going to win. Unless—and this was Lindsay's only play—the girl somehow messed it up so egregiously that even "Aunt Vickie" couldn't possibly crown her the winner.

Chloe was probably going to need a little help with that, though. And Lindsay was nothing if not helpful.

She needed ammo, of course, and was pretty sure she'd find it, or enough to devise a plan, in Chloe's iPhone. It was amazing, Lindsay marveled, settling down on the couch in the common room with a pad and pen, that such a slim device could contain so much of someone's life. She crossed her J.Crew leopard-print pajama-clad legs and got to work.

Item #1: e-mails: There were those Chloe had written, and those recently sent to her. There were an inordinate amount from her mom. The supermodel e-nagged hourly. Interesting that Chloe responded only in the tersest prose. Perhaps the princess-apparent wasn't as close to the reigning queen as everyone assumed.

There was a curious e-mail from a magazine called *Poetry*, a note of encouragement for Chloe's style and subject matter, but ultimately rejecting her latest submission. Lindsay wasn't sure what to make of that, but copied it down just the same.

Item #2: *text messages*: Chloe's obsessive manner of communication. She clearly had a huge crowd of friends, but these were her top five: Liam, Sara, Elie, Madison, and Ashley. Chloe and the others, based on snarky texts, seemed not too fond of whoever this Ashley girl was. Lindsay filed that juicy tidbit away for later.

Item #3: *phone calls*: Most matched up to text-buddies, but there were a few that'd come from an unnamed LA number. Chloe's dad?

Item #4: memos to self: These were written in a self-consciously strange style that Lindsay guessed passed as poetry. Whatever.

And photos. It was always good to place a face with a name. Not easy, though, when Chloe's clique all looked like clones: blond, tanned, fit, superficial.

The most interesting item—and by interesting, Lindsay meant what she could use for maximum damage effect—was Liam Lattimore. In his photos from Chloe's slide show, the curly-haired blond looked more like a sunburned beach bum than a senator's son. He *wasn't* that cute. And judging by his lackluster texts—**Yeah, babe**; **TTYL**; **Miss** u 2;—he wasn't that bright or interesting. Yet Chloe, judging from her poetry-laden texts to the boy, was clearly over the moon for him.

But just how into Chloe was Liam?

Lindsay decided to find out.

Top Model Prep
235 Spring Street
New York, NY 10012
Office of Victoria Devachan
PERSONAL & CONFIDENTIAL
TO MR. LIAM LATTIMORE

Dear Mr. Lattimore:

I come to you with a matter of deep importance. Please keep it confidential. It is essential that no one, especially Chloe Huntley, know about this correspondence. We must be discreet.

Lindsay paused, her fingers hovering over the keyboard of her MacBook. She'd smuggled it out of her bedroom, tiptoeing so as not to wake Alexis and Shiva-Rose. Then she'd hunkered down in the common room, her heart pounding as she worked on this nasty bit of treachery.

For a second, she felt another tremor of guilt, but then she reminded herself that she was just evening the playing field. In truth, she was doing the thirty-nine other students a favor.

The teachers-slash-judges at Top Model Prep had not left her any choice. They all fawned over Chloe, making it clear Charlotte's daughter had it in the bag. Luckily, Lindsay had picked up on Chloe's two weaknesses: Liam and her mother.

This was going to work like a charm.

She wondered if she should keep the letter simpler, just write, "don't tell anyone, especially Chloe"? She'd done an excellent job simulating Top Model Prep stationery, now she could only hope the pampered beachboy would understand formal jargon. His texts to Chloe were all written in abbreviations, so she wasn't sure how bright he was. But . . . she had to make this sound official, like it truly was coming from the head of the school. She crossed her fingers and plowed on.

It has come to our attention that Ms. Huntley has invited you to visit her this weekend. Unfortunately, such visitations are against the rules. It is nothing personal, I assure you. No student may have guests during the semester. This includes weekends.

Here, Mr. Lattimore, is where the situation gets delicate, and the reason I feel I must reach out to you. Ms. Huntley, due to her social standing, is often not required to abide by our program's standardized rules. For instance, I am sure she never mentioned the no-visitors rule, although she has personally been reminded of it.

The consequences of breaking this rule will be dire. Points will be deducted from her score, leaving her open to the deep embarrassment of early elimination.

I turn to you, Liam. Would you be willing to cancel your trip, find some reasonable excuse to not come to New York City, without mentioning this letter? Staying away is the best thing you can do for Chloe. Which is what we all want for her, as I'm sure you especially do.

Respectfully,

Victoria Devachan

Lindsay reread the letter several times. It had to sound official, but more crucially, she had to get her point across. Liam had to get the message. *Don't come, and don't tell Chloe we contacted you.*

Lindsay had no real reason to believe she could pull this off. Except for this: Liam was a guy. Guys lied to their girlfriends all the time. No way was Liam Lattimore different.

Satisfied, she e-mailed the document to herself. As soon as possible, she'd hit up a FedEx Office to print it out and send it by overnight mail to sunny California.

Chapter Eight
Shopping Spree

Sneaking out was easy. Easier than Alexis thought it'd be.

Top Model Prep had all kinds of rules about leaving the premises: signing out, writing down your destination, and then signing back in. There were lots of columns on the sign-out sheet that was kept in the lobby of their building. Only—and especially on national holidays like the Fourth of July—no one was there all the time to make sure you did sign out.

So, if you didn't sign out, no one expected you back.

And if you bunked with ferociously self-absorbed roommates, so drenched in their own dramas that they never noticed your comings and goings, you could pretty much do whatever you wanted. With a little guile, a lot of gumption, and a plethora of purpose, Alexis found herself free to roam about New York City. Free to acquire the stuff she needed to stay in the game.

They'd had no classes on Independence Day, allowing Alexis to do a lot of exploring by day. At night, the girls had gathered on the roof garden of their building to watch the fireworks and nibble on the fat-free, red-white-and-blue cupcakes Victoria had ordered. As Alexis observed her suitemates and other competitors in their designer outfits, chattering and Twittering into their nifty phones, she knew what she'd have to do the following day.

Yep, she thought, practically bouncing down busy, bustling Broadway on Wednesday morning before class, *"Plan: Summer" is working out way better than I could have imagined.* Destiny was abso-freakin'-lutely on her side. For once.

Every time she left the cool confines of the Top Model Prep residence and stepped into the hot, crowded, sweaty sidewalk, she got a tingling feeling. New York had to be the attention deficit capital of the universe. Her kind of town!

Broadway was SoHo's main drag, and so far as Alexis could tell, open all night, always crowded, and noisy. Diversity ruled, but it was easy to spot the New York natives. They were the ones who walked purposely and fast, like they were speed racing the clock, and always late. Multitasking was in their DNA; they gabbed on cell phones, sipped lattes, pushed strollers, and stepped into oncoming traffic to hail cabs—all at the same time. These people had no fear of the taxis, cars, buses, limos, delivery trucks, even ambulances constantly honking and jostling for advantage on the street. Only tourists observed traffic signals. Native New Yorkers crossed streets not when the light was green, but at any random pause in the traffic action, or upon calculation that they could beat out an oncoming vehicle.

For Alexis, it all meant that no one was looking at her.

So, where to start today's adventure?

She was over the outdoor stalls and kicky kiosks. Sure, they looked inviting, jam-packed with bags, jewelry, scarves, sunglasses, cell phone accessories—and only one person per table to keep an eye on it all. But who knew they weren't authentic? To lift that fine Fendi bag, only to be mocked by Lindsay? Lesson learned. Alexis wouldn't be fooled twice.

So then, upscale Bloomingdale's? The exclusive, trendy department store was high-end, and packed with the kind of designer clothes an up-and-coming model needed.

Or should she do the more downscale, but way funkier, Yellow Rat Bastard? The boutique boasted everything that wasn't cool yet, but would be. Stuff like urban hip-hop tops, skinny jeans, torn skirts, bags, and belts. How NYC would she look wearing a retro silk-screened T-shirt and tiny denim mini?

Then there were shoes to think about. Trendy, like Steve Madden, or UGGs? Or should she go more model-safe, with classic Sigerson Morrison? All had shops within a block or so. But then again, no way could, or should, she forget the Apple Store, overflowing with iPhones, iPods—*everything iWant*!

She paused on the corner of Prince Street while deciding, clutching her roomy new Gucci tote. Bad move. Instantly, she got dinged by two passersby, one a big guy shouldering a backpack, and the other a tall woman swinging three shopping bags. Both were oblivious.

Yeah, Alexis reminded herself, rubbing her arm. *If you really want to fit in, pick up the pace!*

The Apple Store was a light, bright, two-story affair. Salespeople were (how precious) referred to as Geniuses. Seriously. If you needed help, you went to the nearest Genius Bar and got tutored in all things *i*. The store was also crowded, buzzing. And heavy with security. Several unsmiling, beefy dudes wearing suits with name tags hung by the entrance. Alexis thought: *This is where they put the nonGeniuses.*

Alexis was no genius, but she was on a mission. She was a girl constantly dazzled and delighted by stuff, and needed stuff to realize her dream. Too bad she was chronically cash-impaired. But what Alexis lacked in funding, she more than made up for in motivation and skills.

Simple dos and don'ts.

Do make eye contact with security guards.

Do look like a typical shopper, in her case, a trendily dressed teen with her hair in a ponytail, a white iPod earbud in one ear, and a big ol' designer satchel over her shoulder.

Do browse.

Do seem easily distracted.

Do act casual.

Alexis was an excellent actress. She browsed her way through the Mac section, playing with demo keyboards, squeezing her own phone between her shoulder and ear, punctuating a pretend chat with giggles.

She made her way to the iPod section, noting the newer nanos—cool colors this year!—the iPod touch, and the miniscule shuffle. *Good things come in small packages.* That's what her dad used to say. These good things could easily be slipped into her pocket, her purse, the hem of her rolled-up jeans (thank you, Katie Holmes, for bringing those back!).

Alexis caught the eye of one of the Geniuses and asked him to bring her an assortment of iPods. In the end, it came back to acting ability. Alexis picked up a silver nano and a pink one, held them both in one hand, as if she was deciding. She waited until the Genius's back was turned. With her other hand, she scratched the small of her back—and tucked a blue one into the waistband of her jeans.

She strolled some more, watching to sense if she'd been tracked, then made her way to the bathroom and locked the door. Bathrooms were her friends. Adjustments were made. Packaging came off with the help of another tiny accessory, sharp nail scissors.

She exited the Apple Store exactly as she'd entered: a trendily dressed teen, still with the iPod earbud in one ear and the Gucci bag over her shoulder. In all, she'd picked up three sleek little toys. Nifty new nanos for herself, for her brother Pete in the army in Afghanistan, and for her brother Nick, temporarily doing time in juvie.

Next stop: clothes. It wasn't only her roommates — even scholarship-girl Shiva-Rose outdressed her. It felt as if everyone in the summer program knew how to dress. Alexis could tell she was beginning to stand out, even though most of the girls saw only as far as their own noses.

Still.

The competition would soon thin out. She could not afford to be the obvious imposter. As a kid, Alexis used to sing the song about "one of these things is not like the other." Little kids never think they'll end up being the one that doesn't belong.

Besides, she rationalized in the Bloomingdale's dressing room, expertly removing tags and sensors off a lime green Michael Kors dress like the one her neighbor Jana often wore to class, this situation was totally temporary. Necessity is the mother of invention: a cliché courtesy of Mom. What would her mom, long gone, think of her inventiveness? She pushed the question away.

As soon as her modeling career took off, Alexis would gladly pay for everything. Then *she* could set the trends, she thought as she loped out of the dressing room, instead of scrambling to copy what everyone else wore.

Her shop-op accomplished, everything fitting neatly into her Gucci bag, Alexis ambled north, up Broadway. She crossed crazy-busy Houston Street — which was usually pronounced like the Texas city, Hyu-ston, but in this case, and only in New York, and only for this street, House-ton — passing the big Crate & Barrel, a cute Mexican restaurant, coffee shops, art galleries, and boutiques.

A few blocks up, the shops gave way to apartment buildings, the briefcase carriers to backpack toters, stroller-pushing nannies to book-carrying coeds, shoppers to students.

She didn't have to read the flags hanging above building entrances to know she was no longer in SoHo, but had stumbled upon NYU.

New York University, the college whose campus was in New York's Greenwich Village, or simply, "the Village," as Lindsay referred to it.

What Alexis knew about NYU: It was famous for its film school and former attendees Mary-Kate and Ashley. It was a private school, hugely expensive.

And this: She'd never go there. It wasn't just the money, or her average grades. No one in her family had been to college, a streak that, even after she became a highly paid model, Alexis was unlikely to break.

Then, her eyes fell on a stringy-haired woman on the sidewalk, her top tattered, her rounded back pressed against the building facade. Emotionless eyes flicked up at Alexis. The crude cardboard sign next to her read: HELP ME, HUNGRY. JOBLESS MOM.

Alexis froze. She swallowed, and without thinking, opened her bag, pulled out her wallet, and stuffed a bunch of one-dollar bills into the paper cup in the woman's hand. It wasn't until Alexis righted herself that it hit her: She was the only one who'd stopped. Most of the blithe pedestrians, these privileged students and passersby, never even paused.

Fighting back tears, she continued her walk. Behind her, she heard a voice. The deep timbre of a boy voice. "That was nice of you."

She glanced over her shoulder, blinking tears out of her eyes. And wondered if she was hallucinating.

The boy standing there smiled, a crooked, sheepish smile, and stuffed his hands into his jeans pockets. "Not that many people stop. And it's funny, the ones who do are usually the most raggedy looking—not like you." He gestured to her Gucci bag.

He was tall, at least six-two, wore a loose gray NYU T-shirt, untrendy jeans, and no-name flip-flops.

But there was no mistaking it: Alexis was getting props from billboard-boy.

She wanted to say: *I know who you are*. She wanted to say: *You have me all wrong*. But the only words that made it out, made it out stuttered: "Thank you. I mean, that's nice. . . ."

"Her name is Karen." He shrugged, embarrassed. "I talk to her sometimes. Try and help out." He paused and gave Alexis a shy smile. "I'm Shane," he added, and held out his hand.

Up close, he wasn't the chiseled marble face of the ad, his cheeks not as defined, his nose strong, but not aristocratic. The lips were the same: lush, inviting. And his eyes, dark, heavy-lidded, come-hither sexy, they were definitely the same. As for the rest of him? Impossible to tell, but at that moment? It didn't matter. He had an aura of sweetness and honesty that was impossible to resist.

So Alexis took his hand.

Chapter Nine
Walk This Way

"Good afternoon, beautiful ladies!" Anabelle greeted them with dewy-eyed, theatrical flourish on Thursday.

Lindsay suppressed a yawn, knowing that this class—even if it was taught by the program's kooky "visionary"—had to be taken seriously. The ones they'd had yesterday, on Confidence and Media Training, were filler, like the remaining songs on a CD that came after the really good ones.

This was the first of the classes on runway walking. A prelude to the big finale of Top Model Prep's competition at the end of the August, the Runway Challenge.

The one she had to win.

"In this class," Anabelle said, gesturing with her ringed hands, "you will learn proper posture, appropriate facial expression, how to move, and how to define your signature walk."

"Runway models are human coat hangers," Dan'yel, who was standing beside Anabelle, dead-panned. "And the sooner you embrace that, the better."

Lindsay was actually glad that Dan'yel co-taught this class with Anabelle. Him, she could understand.

"Make no mistake," Dan'yel said seriously, "whatever else you take from this experience, never forget that your *raison d'être* is to show the *clothes* off to their best advantage. On the runway, *you* are incidental to the clothes."

A murmur went through the wide-open space. This classroom reminded Lindsay of an artist's loft, only without the paintings and sculptures. Instead, a long bolt of snow-white fabric, their training runway, was tacked to the floor. On either side, metal folding chairs were arranged to simulate where an audience would be. Today, the girls had taken these seats.

Dan'yel's remarks took some of them by surprise, but not Lindsay. She was an actor, and as any professional knows, the actor disappears into the character she's portraying. On this stage, the clothes were the character.

It wasn't like she'd never worn designer clothes before, either. Lindsay used to have the trendiest threads piled on the floor of her dressing room, thanks to her TV show's wardrobe department and her personal stylist. True, the past years in Staten Island, NYC's least fashion-conscious borough, had seen her clothed mostly by Target. But after she nailed this competition, she'd have her own line *for* Target. She pictured herself doing commercials, urging girls to "get the Lindsay Robinson look, in fashions designed by me!"

"In a few minutes," Annabelle said, "we're going to send two groups into the dressing room. You'll choose something to model from an extraordinary buffet of delectable fashions. We have every big design house represented, as well as pieces from cutting-edge upstarts."

"But"—Dan'yel held one finger up—"for the actual final challenge at the end of the summer, you'll be modeling fashions designed exclusively by one extraordinary woman. And guess what? She just so happens to be here today to help teach this course." He paused, and turned to his right. "I have the pleasure of introducing the freshest talent on the planet, tomorrow's style icon, La Aura B!"

A woman so meek and mousy that Lindsay had assumed she was someone's assistant stood up. Her stringy brown hair fell over birdlike shoulders; her face was obscured by too-long bangs and round hipster glasses. She seemed to be wearing a shawl over a burlap . . . sack?

She was the next-big-thing fashion designer? She looked more like Mary-Kate, the garbage-chic years, only without the supersized latte and the . . . Mary-Kate-ness. Already, Lindsay had a bad feeling about this designer.

"I'm so thrilled that Top Model Prep chose me to work with you," La Aura mumbled. "You are the generation I'm designing for: young, hip, trendsetters."

"I thought we didn't matter, we're incidental to the clothes," Shiva-Rose leaned over and whispered. "Which is it?"

"Oh, please," Lindsay sniffed. "She's as phony as her name."

"La Aura?" asked Shiva-Rose.

"Or, maybe . . . *Laura*?" pronounced Lindsay. "She's probably Laura Boring from Nowheresville."

Chloe threw Shiva-Rose and Lindsay an

admonishing glance, and Lindsay wanted to giggle, remembering the letter she had sent off to Liam yesterday. Alexis, meanwhile, seemed utterly distracted, one hand toying with her red curls while she gazed off into the distance. What was on *her* mind?

"I can't wait to get to know each one of you personally," La Aura purred.

"You can't wait to see which of us make your lame clothes look good," Lindsay interpreted under her breath.

"You don't know her clothes are ugly," Shiva-Rose pointed out practically.

Lindsay shot her a *just wait and see* look.

After meeting the designer, the girls were sent to the dressing room and given fifteen minutes to find an outfit, plus accessories and shoes.

The dressing room was lined with full-length mirrors, and jammed with racks of fashions representing an array of styles. On one rack alone, Lindsay recognized the haute couture of Chanel and Dior mixed in with the whimsical punk of a Stella McCartney snakeskin and a L.A.M.B. leather-and-lace dress. Classic designer-prep from the likes of Burberry's plaid and Calvin Klein's pencil skirts brushed up against the hipster cool look of John Varvatos.

It was a shopaholic's paradise, and judging by squeals of *OMG! Look at this!*, total fantasy fulfillment for the would-be models. They couldn't have been more blown away if Gwen Stefani herself had sailed into the room, or if someone had parted racks and a random Jonas brother popped out.

One full wall of the dressing room was lined with shelves of accessories — sparkly scarves, squishy clutches, wraparound sunglasses — and shelves of peep-toe pumps, platform boots, and sleek ballet flats.

The group attacked the racks and shelves like starving vegans let loose in Whole Foods, but Lindsay hung back. The cornucopia of clothes was kind of a test itself, wasn't it? A model-hopeful should have good instincts for what looks good on her. The instructors were probably waiting to see who'd choose flattering fashion, and who would leapfrog onto planet "What Was She Thinking?"

In exactly fifteen minutes, they were called back to the classroom and directed to the training runway. As a group, they looked like a costume party in search of a theme, each girl having chosen a dramatically different look.

Lindsay had slipped on superhigh silver wedge sandals and a spangled, short-sleeved Stella McCartney minidress, with neon-pink tights. She was confident she'd done well.

She was just as confident that most of her competition had not.

Faye, the girl from across the hall who'd done poorly before, was in a play-it-safe champagne-colored satin gown. Her complexion looked washed out, and the style would have been boring enough without the addition of black . . . pumps? Swizzle-stick Bikini was in a flared, mermaid-style dress, while curvy Ava had chosen horizontal stripes.

Alexis had not done herself any fashion favors, either. The small girl was completely dwarfed by a green feathered dress cinched by a thick black belt. Over her shoulder, she lugged a gorgeous—but clashing—gold Dooney & Bourke satchel. Shiva Rose had settled on a high-necked black ensemble that might have worked for, say, a funeral.

Chloe appeared to have grabbed whatever she was closest to: an orange-and-gold minidress done in cascading waves of fabric. It was supposed to be fringed, but looked more like it'd been through a paper shredder. The dress was a hot mess.

Unfortunately, Chloe Huntley looked amazing in it.

"This is quite the eclectic showing," Dan'yel said, obviously amused. "We'll start by having you line up, one behind the other, taking small steps along the runway. Please listen, and follow our directions on form."

"Keep your eyes focused straight ahead at all times, like you're gazing at your muse," Anabelle told them. "Don't look up, don't look down, don't look around."

"Sounds more like a zombie than a muse." Alexis, in line behind Lindsay, giggled.

"A zombie with feelings," Lindsay caught herself responding goofily.

"One foot in front of the other. Exactly in front of it," Dan'yel instructed as the girls began moving. "Heel to toe, heel to toe."

Lindsay did as instructed—but felt foolish doing it. The walk was not natural, unless you were playing an Olympic gymnast. Or one of the Flying Wallendas.

As if on cue, Dan'yel edified, "Pretend you're on a tightrope. Toes face forward, footprints form a single line. No wobbling."

It wasn't easy! Although Lindsay was doing okay, Alexis was totally wobbling, and La Aura nailed her on it.

"If you can't do it after several tries, you've probably chosen the wrong shoes, or your outfit is too tight and constricting. Today, you had a choice of what to wear. In a real fashion show, you won't, so I suggest practicing in different styles and heel heights."

Anabelle cheered them on. "Keep walking, you're doing marvelously! Shoulders back, pelvis slightly forward. Everyone look at Jana, she's got it perfectly."

Jana? She was pipe-cleaner thin, and wore a skintight red skirt—she barely *had* a pelvis! Fine. Lindsay copied the pose just the same.

"As you walk, I want to see you swing your arms gently but only from the elbows down. Keep your upper arms close in and tight to your body," Dan'yel said.

"Really, dear, is that your natural walk?" La Aura was staring at Shiva-Rose, who turned scarlet. "You look like you're marching! All you need is a tuba."

Lindsay was surprised to feel defensive about her roommate. Granted, on the runway, Shiva-Rose seemed a bit stiff, but she wasn't awful.

"Create beautiful lines with your body, elongate your neck, use your core," Annabelle blathered.

"In a real fashion show, the runway will be on a raised platform, and you'll be tempted to look at the audience below you," La Aura noted. "Don't. Keep your focus straight ahead."

"And at a real fashion show, there will be music blasting, and throngs of photographers. You can't let the cameras distract you," Dan'yel warned. "The flashbulbs will blind you—and, trust me, girls, this has happened: If you can't see, you'll keep walking—and fall right over the edge of the platform."

Falling off the platform. Hmmm. Lindsay liked the sound of that. For Chloe.

Abruptly, the models were sent back to the dressing room to change. This time, they were given only ten minutes to disrobe, chose another outfit, and return to the runway. In the end-of-summer competition, they were reminded, they'd have even *less* time between changes. Might as well get used to being speedy.

"Of course," Lindsay said aloud to anyone listening, "in a real competition, the backstage area would be swarming with assistants. People would be helping us in and out of preselected outfits—we wouldn't waste time pawing through racks and dressing ourselves."

"True," Chloe said breezily, "but in a real competition, you need to factor in hair and makeup changes for each outfit. And do it all in under three minutes to keep the runway pace."

"You're just a font of information. Memo to self: Find time to worship the ground Chloe and her five-inch heels teeter on," Lindsay shot back as she scoured the racks. She picked out a strapless plum-colored dress with a toile skirt that she knew would look lovely on her.

Shiva-Rose, clearly rattled by Lindsay's obnoxious comment, nearly ripped her mournful black ensemble rushing to get it off. Lindsay would have handed the girl a glittery halter top to show off her broad shoulders. Something by Isabelle Toledo, who famously designed for First Lady Michelle Obama.

But Lindsay stopped herself from intervening. To help someone else was self-sabotage. At the end of the day, this was a competition.

Something Lindsay Robinson had been doing all her life, and excelled at — when she had an audience. When she was eight years old, she competed against more experienced and well-connected kids to win the role of D'Neese on *Yes, We Blend.*

Off-camera, she'd been a bit sullen, an underdeveloped kid with unpredictable hair. But once the cameras rolled, Lindsay came alive. She lit up the room. She was bright and funny, loveable even when delivering snarky lines. She'd been an instant kid star.

Big perks came with big fame. Free clothes and shoes, the hottest new video games and cell phones. She got to see movies before anyone else did, in private screening rooms. The best part was being fawned over every time she went out, asked for autographs, to pose for pictures with fans, treated with deference. And she was making a ton of money.

The big problem with big fame: It had the lifespan of a flea. Once it was over—in her case, puberty, braces, and weight gain felled her—it was like it never existed. She got drop-kicked back into the swarm of school, nondesigner fashions, and anonymity.

But Lindsay would get back to the top, no matter what it took. As a celebrity, she was *someone.* Otherwise, who was she?

No one she wanted to know.

Back out on the runway, decked out in new fashions, they practiced what they'd learned so far. Few of the girls looked comfortable, Lindsay noted.

"You, the girl in the plum sundress," La Aura spoke.

"Me?" Lindsay asked, turning around proudly.

"Lose the cocky expression. You're not embodying the dress. That's not what the dress is saying," La Aura said.

"What's it saying, then?" Lindsay snapped.

"It's shouting for you to dial it down," La Aura said. "It's a simple, delightful fun frock, not a stuck-up movie star ensemble." And then La Aura added, "Take a tip from Chloe. Her outfit says trendy, and her compassionate expression gives her layers of complexity."

Was she *kidding*? Chloe, pale as paste, wore no expression at all. She'd chosen another shredded ensemble, black with random patches of lace and fringed cap sleeves.

Too late, Lindsay understood.

Everyone assumed Chloe had chosen her outfits randomly, but not even. Both changes had been fashions by . . . guess who? La Aura B.

Despondent, Lindsay wondered if her little Liam plan would even work; Chloe seemed smarter than anyone gave her credit for.

Chapter Ten
Best Face Forward

She hadn't heard from Liam all day, and Chloe hated to admit it, but she was stressing.

And stressing was *so* not good for the class she was walking into now—Makeup. Stress meant perspiration and pimples. Chloe rarely, if ever, broke out, but if anything could cause her to do so it was Liam not responding to her texts. It was Friday, and he was supposed to show up tonight, or tomorrow at the latest. What was going on?

"Why do we even *need* this class?" Lindsay challenged Victoria as soon as the girls were seated in their swivel chairs. "In the real world, we'll always have makeup artists."

Au contraire, Chloe could have said, but that was Victoria's job, and she let her do it. Makeup was the only class Victoria herself taught alongside the school's chief creative artist, Dan'yel.

"As an up-and-coming model, you must know how to do your own makeup." The former supermodel said exactly what Chloe knew she would. "You have to be familiar with all the tools, and carry them with you at all times. You have to know what looks best on you in different lights. You have to learn to cover up"—she paused—"imperfections."

Chloe knew what Victoria meant. Blemishes, undefined cheekbones, dark under-eye circles, blotchy skin, short lashes, thin lips, or over-plucked brows. In Chloe's expert assessment, there were few examples of absolute perfection at Top Model Prep—present company excluded. She wasn't being arrogant. Having inherited the porcelain complexion, saucer eyes, pert nose, and lush-lipped beauty specific to fashion models did not make her feel superior. Only trapped.

Her iPhone chirped softly, and she glanced down, her heart in her throat.

To: Chloe From: Mom

How'd u sleep?
When's 1st competish?
Spoken to Aunt Vic?

Send

Things Chloe hated: her mom using "cool" text abbreviations. Her mom pestering. Her mom texting.

And the fact that Liam still hadn't gotten in touch.

Today's class was being held in Top Model Prep's hair salon and makeup studio. It was impressive, with four walls of lightbulb-framed mirrors and marble countertops covered with the best brands of lip gloss, eyeliner, and blush, as well as brushes, tweezers, and swabs. The effect was like someone had raided Sephora, M·A·C, and the Bobbi Brown boutique at Bloomingdale's, and dumped it all here.

Chloe had practically grown up in places like this, watching her mom being powdered, pampered, and primped to someone's idea of perfection. Her mom would arrive with her "real" face, pretty and pale. After being ministered to by hordes of brush-wielding "artists" and assistants, she'd come out with Charlotte Huntley's cover girl–worthy face.

Chloe used to think of it as being defaced, then refaced. She never understood what was so great about it.

Sometimes, she'd curl up beneath the counter with a book on her lap. Invariably, one of the makeup artists would give her a tube of lipstick to "color" with. But Chloe wasn't playing with coloring books, never had. As soon as she could read, it was storybooks, fairy tales, unicorns and princesses, all the time. The kingdoms, forests, and enchanted lands inhabited by those characters were so much more preferable to her own, some would accuse, fairy-tale existence.

"The first part of today's class will be devoted to skin," Victoria told them.

"That's deep." Alexis leaned over, lowering her voice. "Get it? Skin-deep?"

Chloe shot her a small smile. Alexis wasn't half bad. In other circumstances, she might have even been part of Chloe's crowd. But the girl had to learn to dial it down! Over sushi last night, she'd gushingly confessed to Chloe that she'd *met,* and actually *touched*, the underwear model from the billboard. His name was Shane, and he was a student who modeled on the side. She could not stop raving about how amazing he was, how considerate, how sweet. Chloe knew that the boy-model—even if he *was* into girls—was probably not going to be Alexis's knight in shining armor. Midwest-Girl had a lot to learn.

Still, there was something about Alexis's unbridled enthusiasm that was refreshing. With the right makeup and clothes—and in spite of being height challenged and freckled—Alexis could be the dark horse, the bold, unexpected choice, to be Top Model.

Maybe Chloe would even help her.

"No one has perfect skin," Dan'yel was saying, "so let's start by helping you determine what type you have, how to make your best choices."

"Love the skin you're in?" chirped Bikini, mimicking a commercial.

Victoria extolled the virtues of overall skin care: Eat healthy, get enough sleep, never drink alcohol, say no to drugs, don't smoke cigarettes or overstay your welcome in the sun, no matter how much sunscreen you slather on.

Chloe stifled a yawn.

"Pu-leeze don't get insulted," Dan'yel warned them, "but we will be using some of you as examples of oily or dry skin or uneven complexions. It doesn't mean anything's wrong with you. You're here to learn, and no one is being singled out."

Chloe knew that was a lie. Everyone would be singled out, humiliated, publicly embarrassed, shot down for something. They hadn't been here a week, and it'd already happened to Shiva-Rose and that girl Faye, among others. What masquer-aded as "constructive criticism" usually felt like a punch to the gut. Those girls who really wanted to model, who were determined to work their bony butts off, might as well learn it now: They were in for a world of criticism, often laced with sarcasm and sometimes meanness.

What had been drummed into Chloe from her mom: Take direction and make corrections. When the photographer says, "thrust out your chest," act like he's not implying you're flat-chested. When the direction is, "suck in your pelvis," pre-tend not to hear the implicit criticism about your weight.

It took practice.

Grow a thick skin, remain stick thin.

That was the golden rule of modeling.

"Shiva-Rose," Dan'yel called, "please come up here where everyone can see you."

Chloe cringed on behalf of her roomie. She had noticed that Shiva-Rose sometimes got breakouts on her T-zone, but it was nothing too terrible. Still, she knew Victoria would not go easy on the girl.

"Oily skin must always be kept scrupulously clean. You especially need to use clay masks, loofahs, and exfoliate daily," declared Victoria, cupping Shiva-Rose's chin in her delicate hand and eyeing her critically.

Chloe rolled her eyes. What was Victoria implying? That Shiva-Rose didn't wash her face enough? Lots of people broke out in zits, especially under pressure. How was putting her in the spotlight helpful, exactly?

And then Chloe surprised herself—by interrupting the lesson.

"You know, Victoria, sometimes my own forehead gets oily but the rest of my face is flaky and dry. What do you suggest for uneven skin?"

Victoria was taken aback by Chloe's borderline rudeness. Another instructor might have said, "We'll get to that later," but not Victoria, she knew where her croissants were buttered. When Charlotte Huntley's daughter specifically asked for attention—even after claiming she didn't want it—you gave it.

"Of course, Chloe." Victoria gave her a tight-lipped smile. "Come up here and we'll demonstrate."

Meanwhile, she told Shiva-Rose to practice with cleanser. "Work with Ava over there. She also has oily skin."

Rescued, Shiva-Rose could not get away fast enough. She broke for the other side of the room, where Ava was toying with bronzing powder.

Chloe kept Victoria occupied by asking questions about tanning salons and acting like this was the first time she'd ever heard about the care and cleansing of uneven skin. She snuck a glance at Shiva-Rose, who was now laughing with Ava over a shade of ruby red lipstick. Chloe was struck with a realization. This was the first time she'd seen Shiva-Rose genuinely smiling. The first time she'd seen this roommate lighten up, loosen up.

When Victoria was through with Chloe, she sent her back to her seat, and turned the discussion to lip plumping.

Which instantly sent Chloe's mind back to Liam. And, specifically, to *his* lips. Together, they made magic, her pouty lower lip just under his curvy upper lip, trading kisses for hours on end.

Chloe felt a flash of pain. She'd read that amputees felt the worst pain in the part of their body that was no longer there. She totally got that now. Liam was her missing part.

"Chloe?" Alexis summoned her back to reality. "What you did for Shiva-Rose. Very cool."

Chloe shrugged. Someone else might have said, "I know what it's like to be picked on." But Chloe had never experienced that, and didn't pretend to. She had no idea why she'd rescued Shiva-Rose, but was satisfied with the outcome.

"Are you thinking about Liam?" Alexis guessed, her eyes wide. "I'm thinking about Shane," she whispered with a guilty grin.

Chloe couldn't help but smile as the girls around her got up and headed for the counters to practice applying makeup. "I am. I can't wait to see him."

"So what time is his flight coming in?" Alexis asked.

"There's no set schedule," Chloe replied, wishing Liam *was* a little more scheduled when it came to seeing her. "It's his family's private plane, so whenever he gets a crew together."

"That must be nice." Alexis sighed. "Knowing you'll be seeing the boy you love so soon."

Chloe chewed on her bottom lip, shaking off a feeling of foreboding. *Let's hope that happens*, she thought.

Chapter Eleven
Not a Date

It wasn't a date, Shiva-Rose told herself sternly. And it wasn't breaking any Top Model Prep rules, since as far as she knew, there weren't any barring an instructor and student from just going for a walk and grabbing some Jamba Juice.

Only that's not exactly what Shiva-Rose and Mack Scarborough were doing.

The Saturday after their first full week of classes, the two of them were together on a ferryboat headed past the Statue of Liberty. Mack was taking pictures. And Shiva-Rose was having . . . kind of . . . a really good time.

The day had started innocently, if clumsily. They'd happened to bump into each other getting breakfast in a SoHo café. Mack was in line, talking to the server, deciding between a healthy egg-white omelet and a huge buttery brioche. He'd looked cuter than ever with sunglasses on top of his head and his camera gear strapped around his body.

It'd been Shiva-Rose who'd stopped at his side with a flippant suggestion, "Why not have both?"

She'd taken him by surprise. He'd spun around, knocked his tray into hers, which caused hers to tilt upward, sending her coffee and guidebook flying, and his clattering to the floor altogether, orange juice splattering everywhere.

"Oh, I'm so sorry." Mack seemed more annoyed at himself than embarrassed.

Shiva-Rose felt embarrassed enough for both of them. But all she'd done was make a comment—what was he so jittery about?

Unless Lindsay's snarky comments had been right . . .

No. She felt herself blushing. She couldn't go there.

"No worries," she said, setting her own tray down and kneeling to pick up the cups.

"I got you soaked," he'd said. "Not cool."

"An accident." She'd shrugged as he helped her to her feet, offering her a bunch of napkins.

"I owe you a new top. You've got orange juice stains all over you."

"Orange is a good color for me?" That was lame. She'd flushed and turned away suddenly, unwilling to be pinned by his piercing eyes. "Besides, it'll come out in the wash," she'd added.

"Here." He'd handed her the Lonely Planet guide to New York, the book that'd fallen off her tray. She'd meant to thumb through at breakfast for sightseeing ideas. Before leaving the suite, she'd asked Alexis to come with her, but the freckled sprite had begged off, citing other (mysterious) plans.

"What were you going to do today?" Mack had asked casually, his fingers grazing hers as she took the book from him.

"I don't know yet. I was about to read this and decide."

"What have you seen so far?"

Aside from the chocolate shop, which she could have seen at home, not much, she'd admitted. Not that she was in New York to play tourist, but it was Saturday, and she was looking forward to walking around.

"Can I make a suggestion?" he'd asked, his full lips curving up in a smile. Shiva-Rose felt her heart skip a beat, and she'd nodded. "One of my favorite things to do is head down to Battery Park, on the tip of Manhattan, and take a ride on the Staten Island Ferry—"

"Staten Island?" She cut him off. "My roommate Lindsay is from there."

"Don't let her hear you say that!" He'd smiled, and Shiva-Rose couldn't suppress a chuckle. "Lindsay is a legend in her own mind," Mack had said, "but that's okay. You need an extra helping of confidence to make it in this field."

"She's got that covered." Shiva-Rose had agreed, surprised by Mack's perceptiveness.

"So anyway, the ferry. You get the most amazing views of the Statue of Liberty, Ellis Island, and Governor's Island, *and* it's free."

"Wow, sounds cool," Shiva-Rose had said, feeling nervousness bloom in her as Mack studied her intently. She'd fumbled in her messenger bag for her cell phone, thinking out loud. "Um, Alexis said she had other plans today, and Chloe's waiting for her boyfriend to arrive, and Lindsay would never agree to something so touristy—"

"I'll go with you," Mack had said, a smile lighting up his face. "I don't have any other plans, and I owe it to you after making this mess. We can pick up some Jamba Juices to go and take the subway downtown."

Shiva-Rose had swallowed hard. Never had she seen a guy with such huge, mesmerizing eyes. Thinking of Rahm's basic brown eyes back home, there was no comparison. Mack's eyes were green, flecked with yellow, and framed by the darkest, lushest, longest lashes; they were like a weapon. A girl got caught at her own peril. Fighting was futile.

So that was how Shiva-Rose found herself on this ferry, under the gray, threatening skies of New York City, with Mack Scarborough as her companion.

The boat was crowded with tourists; apparently Mack wasn't the only one who knew about the city's biggest bargain. Many had opted to take seats in the indoor part of the boat, clearly scared off by the clouds. That seemed silly to Shiva-Rose. Why get on the ferry if you weren't going to be outdoors, watching the boat's bow split the foamy water as it left the terminal? Even if it did rain, so what? It was only water.

Mack steered Shiva-Rose to the front of the boat, very *Titanic*-like—if not for the other people in the same area. He was not, thankfully, pretending to be King of the World, or trying to kiss her.

He was, however, taking pictures of her, and Shiva-Rose didn't know what to say about that, so she tried to ignore it. She breathed in the salty air, took in the sights. She let the breeze billow her hair, threatening all sorts of knotty tangles, and she went to tie it back. But Mack asked her not to.

"Let me take a few more pictures first, at least," he said from behind the lens.

She bit her lower lip. "I'm not really comfortable with that," she finally said.

"Why not?" He was still behind the viewfinder, framing her against the sky. In the distance, the Statue of Liberty stood proud.

"You're my—our—instructor. The photo competition, where people get eliminated, is only a week away. It doesn't feel, I don't know, right."

Mack put the camera down. "One thing has nothing to do with the other."

"Well, it kind of does," Shiva-Rose argued. She was a big believer in fairness. Maybe someone like Lindsay, who clearly believed that all was fair in love and war, would be cool with being photographed by Mack outside of class. Shiva-Rose was not.

"Exquisite," he said, behind the lens again.

Oh, this is not good.

"Lady Liberty," he said, nodding at the most famous statue in the world as they passed by it.

Shiva-Rose spun around. Whoa! He wasn't kidding. The statue, never mind the hordes of tourists lined up before it, was fierce, powerful, and, to her surprise, it elicited an emotional response from her. She knew the history of course, but being up close was different. And much more meaningful than the Fourth of July fireworks or the view from the rooftop of SoHo House had been.

"I'll make a print of you with the statue in the background," Mack offered, clearly seeing how moved she was. "You can send it to your family back home. I'll even buy you a cheesy frame to put it in. And some dippy Statue of Liberty tchotchke to go with it."

Shiva Rose grinned at Mack's precise pronunciation of the Yiddish word for knickknacks.

He grinned back. "Living in New York," Mack told her, "everything rubs off on you, words from other countries. You don't even think about it."

"Have you always lived here?" Shiva-Rose asked.

He shook his head. "Army brat."

"Really?" That was interesting. Being as she'd one day be in the Israeli army.

"My old man got transferred from base to base, so I never stayed in one place too long," he said, continuing to take pictures of Shiva-Rose with Ellis Island in the background and with Governors Island opposite her, surrounded by clouds above and sea below.

"How'd you end up here?" Shiva-Rose wanted to know. "In this job?"

"I was insanely motivated. Constantly moving, changing schools, the strict, rigid atmosphere at home was tough. I wanted to get as far away from that scene as fast as I could. No offense."

"None taken." Shiva-Rose's military duty was mandatory, but she'd have chosen to do it anyway.

She had a different life and didn't expect outsiders to understand. "Did you go to university in New York? Is that how you got the Top Model job?"

"I had a mentor who lived here. She was famous for shooting rock stars. I sent her my portfolio and she allowed me to apprentice," he replied, ducking her question about school. "Getting the Top Model gig was sheer luck."

"And talent." Shiva-Rose surprised herself by saying it. The last thing this guy needed was another ego stroke.

"Thanks." At least he managed to sound borderline humble.

"Can I ask you something?" She didn't wait for an answer. "That day in class, when you reamed out Faye for her flower interpretation . . . why did you do that?"

Mack stopped shooting, and set his gaze off in the distance. "How could I be so cruel? Is that your question?" Shiva-Rose shrugged, and Mack took his time responding. "Faye has real promise. Potential. I know I wasn't diplomatic. I probably hurt her feelings. But if she's going to make it as a model, and I believe she can, she's going to have to learn to take criticism."

"Even if it's harsh," Shiva-Rose added. "But what about the others?" She meant Jana. Bikini. Ava. "You weren't happy with their poses, either, but you weren't so hard on them."

Again Mack took his time responding. "They need seasoning."

"In other words, they're ditzy."

"Hey, you said it, not me!" He put his palms up defensively, but his eyes were sparkling.

At the Staten Island terminal, they boarded a Manhattan-bound ferry. Above them, the blanket of clouds finally gave way to rain. Most of the other passengers immediately went inside for cover. But the rain didn't bother Shiva-Rose. In fact, she found the rainfall cleansing somehow. If Mack hadn't been there, she might have given in to impulse and tipped her chin up, opened her mouth to capture the droplets.

"Be right back," Mack said, heading toward the interior of the boat.

Shiva-Rose gripped the railing and stared out at the choppy gray water. How strange to be spending the summer on an island when she'd spent her entire life in a desert. How strange that at this moment, she wasn't homesick.

She sensed Mack's return before he said anything. He'd come up directly behind her, had left little room between them. She tensed, feeling his breath on her neck, slowly twisted her head around—and giggled.

Mack Scarborough, hipster-photographer and girl-magnet, looked like a duck! He was covered in a canary yellow rain slicker from head to toe, the words STATEN ISLAND FERRY emblazoned across his chest. He'd also brought one for her.

Still giggling, Shiva-Rose extended her arms and allowed him to slip the rain poncho over her head.

"That was thoughtful of you, thanks."

"Here, wait." He pulled the hood up so it covered her hair. Let his forefinger linger on her cheek.

She didn't stop him.

Gently, he traced her jawline, brushing a stray hair off her cheek, onto her neck. In that one tender moment, Mack Scarborough stepped over the line from quasi-innocent flirting to something much more.

Conflicting emotions instantly set up camp inside her. She wanted to move in closer, melt into his arms. But that would be wrong. In so many ways. But . . . it was nice to feel close to someone when she was so far away from everyone she loved.

And he was so beautiful.

Resolve, reality, doing the right thing won out. She moved her head away from him.

"I'm not comfortable with this," she said stiffly, echoing her earlier sentiment.

He moved his hand away. "Because I helped you put on a rain slicker?"

Don't play dumb.

"Because this program is important to me. It's my future. I can't afford to— "

"Make a friend?"

You know what you did. And you know I liked it.

"Not that kind of friend, not with my instructor, no. And you're probably way too old for me."

"Can you keep a secret?" Mack leaned in even closer, whispered in her ear.

Shiva-Rose said nothing, kept her eyes straight ahead. They were almost back at the terminal in Battery Park City, where they'd started.

"I told them I was twenty-five. To get the job. No one checked."

Now Shiva-Rose looked him in the eye.

"I'm only eighteen."

What just happened?

Guilty and elated, confused, conflicted, and—yes—still tingling, Shiva-Rose tried to sort out her feelings. After making his confession on the ferry, Mack had parted ways with Shiva-Rose back at the terminal. He'd simply touched her arm and said he'd see her in class, but she could tell he didn't want to push the limits by giving her a hug.

Shiva-Rose couldn't bear the thought of returning to the apartment without first digesting what had happened. And she'd signed out of school for the day, so no one expected her back anyway. Soggy guidebook in hand, she figured she'd take in the historical sights of lower Manhattan, buildings dating back to the 1700s, statues of famous heroes, plaques explaining conquests in the fight to free America from British rule. She tried to follow the map and absorb what she was reading.

But like the dense, dizzying side streets that wound through the oldest district in the city, her thoughts kept circling back to Mack.

Had she cheated by going out with him? Not really. They'd gone sightseeing together, but that didn't make it a date. But who was she fooling? Being with Mack had come awfully close.

He could completely influence the scoring of the competition. So it *was* wrong, a bad choice on both their parts to go out together. No matter how good it felt. No matter that she'd felt genuine happiness, even laughed without restraint, for the first time since she'd gotten here.

It wasn't right. She'd win, or not win, playing by the rules. That's who she was.

New rule: No more hanging out with Mack. Stay on task. Focus.

It was close to seven P.M. by the time she returned to the Top Model Residence, drenched in spite of the ridiculous raincoat, deflated because of her decision.

"Hi!" Faye happened to be in the elevator, laden with plastic shopping bags full of delicious-smelling takeout.

Shiva-Rose's mouth watered. That Jamba Juice had been her only meal today.

"I'm catering dinner," Faye informed her. "So

if you don't have other plans, come join us. It's Chinese."

"I love Chinese food," Shiva-Rose admitted, "and I'm starving."

"Excellent! Invite your roommates," offered Faye. "Even Lindsay and Chloe."

They exchanged knowing smiles as they exited the elevator.

Shiva-Rose had the overwhelming urge to confide in Faye, to tell her what Mack had said about her on the boat. To explain that he'd been mean to her because he believed in her, that she had amazing model potential.

But telling her would mean admitting she'd been with him, with their teacher, who obviously favored her, and was, by the way, eighteen. Alone with the guy who could take amazing photos of her, help her ace the competition. Even though she resolved it wasn't going to happen again.

Shiva-Rose ducked into 14C, hoping to find her roommates and invite them to dinner with the 14A girls.

Lindsay, wearing yoga pants and a loose tank top, was curled up in the common room, watching a DVD. She turned it off the minute Shiva-Rose walked in.

"Were you just watching *Yes, We Blend*?" Shiva-Rose asked.

"Did you fall overboard?" Lindsay said uncharitably, pointing at the Staten Island Ferry slicker.

"No, I was out in the rain. Listen, they invited us for takeout next door. Are you the only one here?"

"Chloe's here." Lindsay hooked a thumb toward Chloe's closed door.

Shiva-Rose arched her eyebrows. "Oh, so did you meet the famous Liam?"

"He never showed." Lindsay didn't even try to hide the self-satisfied smirk.

Shiva-Rose took off her poncho, her heart contracting at the memory of Mack's touch. Then she headed into Chloe's room to find the blond beauty slumped on the bed, her head resting on her elbow.

"Go away," she mumbled. "Not in the mood for company."

"Did he say why?" Shiva-Rose asked softly as she perched on the edge of the bed.

Chloe shrugged. "I don't know. Something about the plane. Whatever."

This was a Chloe she'd not seen before. There was no hiding the hurt in her eyes, and Shiva-Rose felt a bolt of empathy. "The weather's really bad," she said. "I bet there are huge delays with flights." Chloe said nothing, but Shiva-Rose plowed on. "It's supposed to clear up tomorrow. Maybe he'll show up then?"

"Maybe," Chloe muttered halfheartedly.

Shiva-Rose finally managed to talk Chloe into heading across the hall for dinner. And where a glum Chloe went, a delighted Lindsay was sure to follow. The 14C trio sat down with Faye, Bikini, Jana, and Ava, and attacked a smorgasbord of yummy. The coffee table in 14A's common room was covered with containers of dumplings, soups, beef with broccoli, General Tso's chicken, white and brown rice, and tofu lo mein. The girls had set out paper goods, napkins, iced tea, Diet Coke, and bottles of water.

"How much did you spend on all this?" asked Shiva-Rose, helping herself to the lo mein. "I'll chip in."

"Nada," Faye responded, handing Chloe a pair of chopsticks.

"How many calories are we spending?" Lindsay, ever sarcastic, asked.

Chloe stuffed a fried dumpling into her mouth. "Do you think Faye is sabotaging you with high-calorie food?"

"Not to worry," Faye said. "I told them no MSG, no salt, no butter—"

"OMG!" Chloe suddenly exclaimed—her mood shift from just a short while ago was dramatic. "This tastes just like the diced squab, bamboo shoots, and mushrooms in a lettuce wrap at Mr. Chow! It's this place in Beverly Hills that's really famous and expensive—"

"Or—" Lindsay cut her off, pointing a chopstick at one of the plastic shopping bags the food came in "—it *is* Mr. Chow." She paused. "New York location."

"Faye's aunt owns it," Bikini declared.

Everyone gazed admiringly at Faye, who was about to respond, when the door to 14A swung open and Alexis, wearing a Miu Miu flower-print sundress and peep-toe pumps, swept into the room.

"Sweet! It smells amazing in here. I'm famished! Did you leave some for me?" Alexis flopped down on the floor next to Shiva-Rose, folded her legs under her, and grabbed a plastic fork.

"I see you wised up," said Lindsay, gesturing at the enormous gold bag Alexis had dropped on the floor. "You obviously learned to tell an original apart from a fake. Kudos."

Shiva-Rose followed Lindsay's gaze. How did Alexis come by the exact same ginormous Dooney & Bourke bag that had been on the accessories shelf during runway class? Weird.

Alexis's fork, on which she'd speared something steaming and triangle-shaped, froze midway between the aluminum tin and her mouth.

Suddenly, Faye leaped out of her seat. "Don't eat that!"

"But I love shrimp toast!" Alexis scrunched her forehead.

"Shrimp toast!" Bikini, Ava, and Jana started to laugh hysterically. Faye was obviously tripping all over herself, trying not to be mean, but she couldn't help it. The situation was so silly, the laughter infectious. Lindsay snorted tea through her nose, and even formerly morose Chloe burst out laughing.

Faye gently explained. "It's not shrimp toast. It's a terry-cloth towel. It's steaming hot because they toast them and fold them in triangles to be fancy." She opened it up to show a fiercely blushing Alexis.

"Hey, shrimp toast, want some cardboard box to go with that?" Lindsay jibed. Which set off another wave of laughter. And Shiva-Rose realized it was the first time the model-hopefuls had really relaxed and had fun.

The 14C girls went back to their own suite an hour or so later, satiated and tired.

"Where's Liam?" Alexis asked Chloe, glancing around eagerly.

Chloe visibly tensed. "He'll be in first thing tomorrow."

"You sure about that?" Lindsay said, reveling in her ability to rub salt into the wound. "Usually when a guy puts something off—say, coming to see you—it's because he has no intention of doing it at all."

"In your case, I can see why," Chloe snapped back.

Shiva-Rose high-fived Chloe. It was a good comeback. Too bad it backfired, as Lindsay turned her spiteful spirit on Shiva-Rose.

"And where you were all day? And who were *you* playing King of the World with on the Staten Island Ferry?"

What?

Shiva-Rose felt her heart stop, and she blushed furiously.

How could Lindsay know?

"I thought it might be Mack," Lindsay said with gotcha satisfaction. "I hope you at least got some good photos out of it."

"Good for you," Chloe said. "If he's the fashion world's next superstar photographer, and he made a connection with you—go for it."

Shiva-Rose forced a smile. "I had no one to go sightseeing with. I bumped into him. It was nothing, less than nothing."

"Hmmm . . . less than nothing. Is that like a double negative making a positive?" Lindsay mused, with a devious twinkle in her eye.

Shiva-Rose had no comeback. She wasn't proud of it, but she had to duck out of any more questions. She turned on Alexis. "And what about you—what'd you do today?"

Alexis shrugged. "I went shopping, and I got stuff to spiff up our apartment. Look." She unzipped and upended her big bag. Out poured tea light candles, decorative picture frames, dried flowers, and bud vases.

And—Shiva-Rose couldn't help but notice—not one sales receipt.

Chapter Twelve
Confrontations and Denials

"I still don't understand why you couldn't come," Chloe said. Below her, an ambulance siren wailed, followed by car horns honking, and the squawks of fire engines. Somewhere there was an emergency. That was the night music of New York City.

Liam, on the other end of the phone—the other side of the country—cleared his throat. "What's that noise?" he asked. "Is your window open or something?"

"I'm not in my room, Liam."

"So where . . . are you?" Was that a catch in Liam's voice? Anxiety? She hoped so. It was late. She hoped he pictured her at a club, flirting with older guys. Or hanging out on the street with a bunch of cool people. She hoped he was cursing himself for not showing up at all.

"I'm outside."

"At midnight?" Liam said. "That's got to be against the rules."

Since when had *he* turned into rules-guy? He'd broken way more than she was capable of counting. "I'm on the roof of our dorm."

Silence.

"It's kind of a New York thing. A rooftop is one of the few places to be alone. It's not like I can drive out to the desert."

More silence. Had she lost the connection?

"You're not . . . I mean . . . how high is the roof?"

"What?" Then it hit her. Wait—no. Liam couldn't really think she'd gone up to the roof to jump! Was he scared? Feeling guilty? For a split second, Chloe let him squirm. Then she came to her senses. Liam actually thought she was so distressed over him she'd contemplate jumping? Was he nuts, or just that full of himself?

True, she was crushed. She'd spent a lonely Sunday waiting in her apartment, and then, in the evening, had received Liam's lame text:

And? She'd waited for more. He couldn't fly commercial? If the coddled only son of US Senator James Lattimore wanted something, he got it. If Liam had wanted to see her, he'd have found a way.

So she'd taken her phone up to the roof to find out why he hadn't.

"Chloe, are you okay?" She forced herself to laugh. "Of course I'm okay, Liam. There's a roof-top garden here, it's quiet, private." Chloe flicked her eyes up at the darkened sky. It was a moonless night. A cheesy thought came to her. *The same sky that covers me also covers him.* "Where are you?" It just occurred to her to ask.

"In the car, on my way home."

Home from where? He didn't say. She wasn't going to be that nagging girlfriend who had to know every move he made. She wouldn't even ask him to come see her next weekend. But she hoped, desperately, that he'd offer. So far, he had not.

"Where is the family Learjet, by the way? Delivering food in Africa, doing state business in DC, or at the repair shop?" She tried to be quippy.

"The plane? It's . . ." He stumbled. "I'm not sure."

Asked and answered. Liam hadn't flown to New York because he didn't want to. Lindsay had nailed it. Chloe felt physically sick.

"Listen, Chlo, I . . ."

"It's cool," she managed. "Catch ya' later." She hung up quickly and pressed her back against the guardrail, willing herself not to cry.

Her phone rang. Liam. She didn't pick up.

He texted,

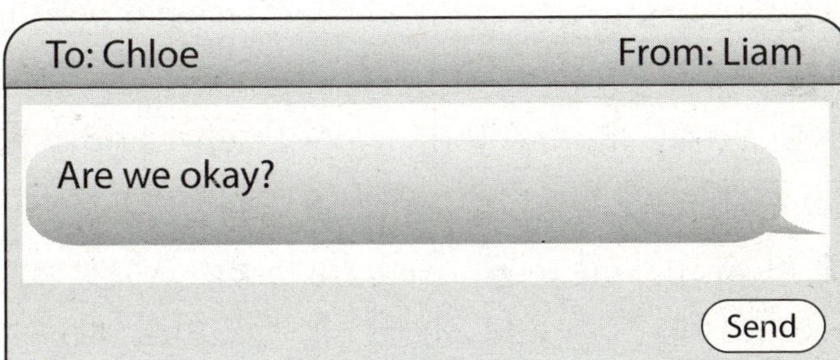

She closed the text without responding. *No, you moron, we are far, far from okay.*

She'd already spoken to her best friends Sara, Elie, Madison, and even annoying Ashley. She knew Liam had spent the weekend at the beach house in Malibu. Same as Chloe's whole crowd had done last week, same as they would do next.

That was summer, Brentwood-style. When Chloe's friends weren't traveling they slept in, then hung out. Either at a sponsored beach house, where paparazzi roamed in hopes of catching a celeb in an ill-fitting bikini. Other times, they stayed at someone's parents' house, where some hookup or another usually happened—although Sara was quick to point out that Liam had been a good boy, a faithful boyfriend. Sara had promised to let Chloe know if anything bad was happening. Then, she'd gone on to fill Chloe in on the daily drama, who was no longer cool, who said what about who, etc.

Chloe sucked in the wet night air. More than once during her calls, she'd been on the verge of talking about life at Top Model Prep. Telling her friends all the failures, jealousy, secrets.

Chloe didn't pay large amounts of attention to her suitemates, but she wasn't totally clueless.

Shiva-Rose was totally on the verge of something inappropriate with Mack; Alexis was sneaking around and acting weird; Lindsay seemed to have a personal vendetta against her.

In less than a week, ten of the forty girls would be gone. If only she could find a way to be in that first group. Right. Like Charlotte was going to let that happen. Her mother, a master manipulator, had doubtless pulled some strings, no matter what Victoria said to the contrary. Chloe was going home no time soon.

Chloe shook her head, shoving her phone in her pocket and leaving the rooftop garden. Would she ever get out from under Charlotte's thumb?

She flung open the fourteenth-floor stairwell door with such force it would have smashed into the wall. Only Alexis caught it, right in the shoulder.

"Ouch! What the—" Alexis yelped in pain.

Chloe's heart hammered. "Oh, no! I'm so sorry, are you hurt?" A bruise was already forming. It'd be purple by tomorrow. But why was she in the hallway at this hour? In a shoulder-baring tank top, short shorts, flip-flops, and a defensive expression.

Alexis massaged her arm, and caught her breath. "I'm fine. You just scared the wits out of me. I didn't expect the door to fly open like that."

"Yeah, the door wasn't expecting you, either. I'm really sorry. But . . . it's after midnight. Are you just getting in?"

"I could ask you the same thing," Alexis said.

Chloe rolled her eyes and explained herself. Alexis did not. Then Chloe did something really stupid. She blocked the door to 14C. "Alexis, really. Where have you been?"

"Are you my mother?" Alexis ducked under Chloe's arm and put the key in the lock. "C'mon, Chloe, so I was out late. It's not a big deal. I'm sure you've been out past curfew once or twice?"

"Not doing anything illegal, I wasn't."

At that, Alexis laughed and morphed into the cute, carefree sprite that probably got her into this competition, and no doubt, would keep her doing well in it. "Go to bed, Chloe. You need your beauty sleep."

She didn't sleep. She was under the covers, eye mask in place, but she kept thinking about Liam. Had he really just ditched her? Out of sight, out of mind? The thought was just too painful. Out of everyone she knew, family included, he was the first person to ever get her. He got that there was more to Chloe Huntley than her looks, her heritage. And for that, she loved him.

Chloe was finally drifting off when a text came in. She bolted upright, grabbing her iPhone. It was from Sara.

To: Chloe From: Sara

Here's the scoop. Liam got a letter and a call from Top Model Prep, some lady there. Told him he wasn't ALLOWED to visit, no matter what you said. Told him it would take points off your score???? Makes no sense to me, but Liam believed it. And I kinda believe him.

Send

Fury and disbelief raced through Chloe. She jumped out of bed, her blood roaring in her ears.

Mom.

What she had done was unforgivable.

Her mom was groggy when she answered the phone.

"Chloe? Is everything all right? What's the matter, baby?"

Chloe got straight to the point. "Why did you do it? Just give me one good reason why."

"Do what?" Her mother sounded genuinely confused.

"Don't pretend you don't know! Don't lie!"

"Sweetheart, I don't know what you're talking about," Charlotte said.

"Yes, you do." Chloe hated sounding whiny and petulant, but she couldn't help it. "You're purposely trying to keep Liam and me apart. That's why you sent me to this ridiculous excuse for a summer program in the first place!"

Her father got on the phone. "You're upsetting your mother. You owe us both an explanation."

Of course he'd say that. Always defending her, taking her side.

"She went totally behind my back—"

"Don't refer to your mother as *she*," her father interrupted.

"Fine." Chloe was seething. "The great Charlotte Huntley, the most beautiful woman in the world, the incomparable—"

"Stop it, Chloe." Her father's voice registered finality.

"*Mom* pretended to be someone from Top Model Prep and told Liam he wasn't allowed to come—to ignore whatever I said. You told him if he showed up they'd take points away from me, and God knows, nothing would be worse for you if I don't win!"

The conversation devolved from there. Charlotte denied everything, denied even knowing Liam and Chloe's plans. But she *wasn't* unhappy about the turn of events. "He's a distraction," she said. "If he's the right one for you, he'll be there when you get back."

Chloe hung up, still shaking. If her mother hadn't orchestrated this, then Aunt Vickie certainly had. Chloe vowed to confront the headmistress first thing in the morning.

Chapter Thirteen
A New Friend

Poor, pitiful Chloe, come so undone by her boyfriend's no-show that she barely limped through classes on Monday. So much planning, texting, lording her "private room" over Lindsay. And when Liam had changed his plans, cool Cali girl Chloe had gotten very hot and bothered under her Burberry collar.

The LA blond tried to hide her feelings beneath that perfect face, but Lindsay knew distraught and disappointed when she saw it—most especially when she herself had caused it.

And early Monday morning—Lindsay had it on good authority—the entitlement queen had stomped into Victoria's office and accused the head of the school of conspiracy! Of conspiring with her mother to keep Liam away.

Word was, the confrontation hadn't gone well. Victoria had been shocked by Chloe's accusation, and more than a little worried about the girl's state of mind.

Score!

Lindsay didn't think she could feel any more satisfied. Her scheme had been genius. Brilliantly executed. After she'd sent the letter to Liam, she'd followed up with a confirming phone call in the guise of Alison Seegle, assistant to Victoria Devachan. Alison didn't exist, but Liam didn't know that.

The unexpected bonus was that Liam never questioned a thing. Not the veracity of the letter, or the phone call. Lindsay figured him for lazy, but who knew he'd turn out to be so gullible? The senator's beach-bum son swallowed Lindsay's lie whole, slurped it down like a jumbo smoothie.

The only glitch, if you could call it that, was creativity-challenged Liam had not come up with a "reasonable" excuse for bailing on Chloe. He didn't tell her the truth and couldn't figure out a convincing lie. He compounded his bungling by telling Chloe's BFF Sara about being barred from visiting Top Model Prep.

Like dominoes falling, Chloe found out, freaked out, blamed her mother, and then Victoria as the culprits.

Naturally, neither confessed.

Eventually, Chloe would have to consider the possibility that Liam just didn't care all that much about his devoted, deserted girlfriend. Didn't love her enough to fly in the face of the "rules" and come anyway.

How heartbreaking for Chloe.

But Lindsay wasn't one to rest on her laurels. With the final challenge less than a week away, it was time to amp up her game.

Today's despondent Chloe could be tomorrow's resplendent Chloe: The girl could rebound. Or, she could simply win in spite of herself. As a model, tragically, Chloe Huntley was that good.

The night Lindsay had filched Chloe's iPhone, after finishing the letter to Liam, she'd made a deliberate new friend.

Ashley Angibou was a wealthy teen who attended Crossroads Academy with Chloe, and based on her texts and e-mails, obviously fancied herself part of the A-crowd. What Ashley didn't know: Behind her back, the others mocked her, set her up to be humiliated.

Lindsay made sure Ashley found out. Ah, the magic of forwarding old text messages! Naturally, Ashley was devastated. And hungry for revenge.

Lindsay had cultivated the friendship by sending the girl gift baskets and the promise of friendship as soon as Lindsay got back to the West Coast. For extra incentive, she'd called on her old friend for a favor. Juliet Rivers had been Lindsay's costar, and a good friend, on *Yes, We Blend.* That Juliet had smoothly made the transition from child star to much-photographed teen starlet rankled Lindsay, but to her credit, Juliet never lorded it over her. Now, Lindsay had asked the actress to hang out with Ashley, take her to a club one night, give her a taste of the really good life.

Between Juliet and Ashley, Lindsay knew Chloe would be done for.

On Tuesday night, alone in the triple, Lindsay picked up the phone and called Los Angeles.

"Hi, Ashley, how are you? Did you get the little gift basket I sent? Great. I have a favor to ask—and I think you're going to get a kick out of this one."

Things between Chloe and Liam were about to get messier, and Ashley was going to have a hand in it.

"What do you need me to do?" Ashley asked, cracking her gum.

"Not a big deal," Lindsay assured her, "a little gossip, a text here, an IM there."

"You'll tell me what to say?" Ashley wanted reassurance. "Exactly what to do?"

"I'll type it out for you. Word for word."

After texting Ashley, Lindsay sighed contentedly and flopped across her twin bed, gazing at Shiva-Rose and Alexis's bunk bed. Shiva-Rose's bed was pin-neat, but it had been obvious in photo class yesterday how messy her emotions were when it came to Mack.

Lindsay had been bowled over when she'd happened to spy Shiva-Rose and Mack on the ferry when she'd been going home to see her 'rents on Saturday. Now she knew that she had to encourage Shiva-Rose to continue her friendship-slash-flirtation with the gorgeous photographer. The result would obviously be better shots of Shiva-Rose than Chloe in the photo challenge.

Lindsay's gaze traveled to Alexis's unmade bed. She had a feeling the sweet-seeming sprite was up to some sketchy stuff, and Lindsay hoped she wouldn't get caught.

At this point, Lindsay needed the pretty little roommate in the game.

Chapter Fourteen
Stealing Away

"Where are you going?"

Alexis froze, turning around outside of the Top Model Residence to see Shiva-Rose striding toward her, holding a plastic salad container from a nearby deli. Dinner. It was Tuesday night, and Alexis was heading out to meet Shane—and do a few other fun things. She was armed with her Dooney & Bourke bag and her Gucci satchel. Both bulged with packages.

"Out," Alexis said flatly, crossing her arms over chest.

"Don't lie to me," Shiva-Rose said, catching Alexis off guard. She took a step closer to her, dark eyes flashing. "I saw you," she added accusingly.

Alexis felt her heart thudding. "I'm not lying. I don't know what you think you saw."

"I saw you stealing. In class today. I saw you taking the clothes off the racks in the back of the dressing room and—"

Alexis was not going to back down.

"And what? If I took anything—and I'm not saying I did—where is it? Care to search my room? Oh, wait, you live there, too."

Shiva-Rose wasn't having it. "What about this bag?" she asked, pointing to the Dooney & Bourke. "Did you really spend, like, five thousand dollars on the exact same bag we happened to have on the accessories shelf? What a coincidence."

"I just borrowed the bag, and forgot to return it." Alexis improvised, wiping her sweaty palms on her jeans. "Big deal. No one even noticed, except you, eagle eye." Alexis had begun to veer from defense to offense.

Shiva-Rose took a deep breath. "I'm worried, Alexis. I like you. I don't want anything bad to happen, that's all."

"Nothing bad is going to happen," Alexis promised.

Suddenly, Alexis wished she could explain herself to Shiva-Rose, come clean. But the international girl, so smart and so focused, saw everything in black and white. There were no gray areas. *Stealing is wrong*, she'd say.

"I'm sure you're just imagining things," Alexis

added, a note of warning in her voice. "Just like I was imagining the way Mack was staring at you in photo class today?" Alexis felt a pang of triumph as Shiva-Rose's face fell.

Lucky for Alexis, Shiva-Rose had her own moral dilemma. His name was Mack Scarborough. Alexis knew that no matter what Shiva-Rose suspected, she couldn't very well rat someone else out for breaking the rules when she herself teetered on the edge of impropriety.

Shiva-Rose muttered something about dinner, then scurried into the building with her salad. Relieved, Alexis turned and continued on her way.

That had been a close call. Which brought the total to two so far. Thanks to her midnight run-in with Chloe on Sunday, Alexis's shoulder was now a lovely purple hue, which had not thrilled the makeup artists or stylists in classes today.

Still, Alexis knew Chloe wouldn't blab. Something must have happened between their midnight mash-up and the following morning, because the platinum princess had been on the warpath ever since. Everyone knew she'd been expecting her prince to fly in on a white Learjet.

Everyone also knew, since Lindsay spread the bulletin like an Ebola virus, that he hadn't shown up. So Chloe clearly had other things on her mind. Whew.

So far, this summer rocked. Getting sent home because someone had caught her would stink. Nor would it be the first time. Alexis had been booted from a few schools due to misunderstandings. But she learned from her mistakes, her life lessons. She was smarter, cagier now.

Proof: She'd been at this for eleven days, mostly without incident. No one knew her clandestine nightly habits.

Clandestine. Alexis liked that word. It implied action, adventure, even romance.

Like the romance she was about to embark on with Shane.

Alexis felt her heartbeat pick up as she reached the Spring Street subway entrance. The day she and Shane had met, when he'd taken her hand in his, they'd fallen into step and ended up going for a walk. Casual easy-flowing conversation had ensued. He was nothing like Alexis might have expected, not flashy, nor full of himself. When not "on the job,"—and he considered modeling nothing more than a side gig, not a career—Shane took summer classes at NYU. He was pretty sure he could transfer the credits to the University of Florida, where he'd be a sophomore in the fall. He had plans even beyond that, the Peace Corps if they'd take him, or Teach For America.

Shane was only in New York for the summer, living in university housing. His dorm situation wasn't so unlike hers, a similarity they'd remarked on. Although two years ahead in school, he was eighteen; she sixteen. Alexis had been careful not to divulge too much about herself. She'd given him only the basics that day. They had, however, exchanged text and e-mail info. And made plans to meet up again tonight.

Alexis descended the steps to the 6-line subway, the very one Jennifer Lopez immortalized on her debut album, *On the 6*. After studying a chart of the color-coded, numbered or lettered routes on her first week in New York, Alexis had figured out the subway system. She had purchased a sleek yellow MetroCard, which she used regularly. On some nights, when the Spring Street subway station was less crowded, she daringly ducked under the turnstile, avoiding the fare. But tonight, she wasn't taking any chances. There were two cops on the platform. She smiled as she sashayed past them.

It was amazing what a cute face, friendly smile, and a carefree air of confidence could accomplish. Not that the police should take up their valuable time with her, but in stores, or restaurants, or, yep, backstage in Top Model Prep's changing areas, no one (besides Shiva-Rose, and only recently) ever questioned her. She didn't look, or act, guilty of anything.

Nor was she. Not really. Seriously, how was it stealing if no one got ripped off? Eventually, those tourists at the chocolate restaurant would realize they'd been charged for two different meals. And? They'd report a mistake, the credit card company would delete the charge. The restaurant would eventually discover the difference in signatures—that's where it would end.

Alexis considered herself one of the most moral people she knew. She'd never cheat to get an advantage, or take anything from a friend. Not even from Chloe, who had so much stuff she probably wouldn't notice if anything went missing. Stealing from someone you knew; that was just wrong. But liberating stuff that didn't belong to a specific person was another story. Alexis did not see the wrong in giving things to people who really needed them. Herself included.

And Alexis needed to fit in. How else would she have a chance in the competition? Winning this summer program was the kind of miracle she'd prayed for. What Alexis Cournos really needed was not to go back to Hamtramck. She needed to stay in New York, make a life for herself. Reinvention was the name of the game.

Alexis shifted her weight to see over the subway platform. The headlights of the oncoming 6 train illuminated the tracks. It screeched to a stop, and she got on. The train was rarely crowded. She always got a seat, a perch from which to observe her fellow travelers.

The faces, forms, and fashions changed nightly, but there was uniformity in how people behaved as the rails rumbled beneath them. People listened to their iPods; read magazines, newspapers, or books; slept; or chatted over the roar of the train. Those without props pretended to read the advertisements over the windows, but were really checking out some cute girl or guy. Alexis found herself in that category most of the time: the checkee. But now that she'd met Shane—even though they hadn't officially gone out yet—she mentally took herself off the market. She was just looking, observing, taking it all in.

And what surprised Alexis night after night: In this most public of places, when people were so exposed, vulnerable, even trapped in a way, everyone acted oblivious, pretending to be in his or her own world. Making actual eye contact was a no-no. Her own early attempts had been met with suspicion, a quick turning away, embarrassment, or guys misreading her, assuming she was flirting with them. She had to be on guard.

People had reason to be jittery in this city. She understood that. Every so often the disembodied voice came over the loudspeaker system, the reminder to keep their belongings in sight at all times. It seemed to Alexis the best thing was to pay attention. Be in the moment, not in your own world.

"Union Square," announced the fembot over the loudspeaker as the train pulled into a station, "Change here for the L, N, R, W, 4, and 5 trains."

Alexis exited, and once on street level, made

for the post office on Broadway. She had packages to mail, and could have gone to the branch right near the Top Model apartments, but thought it best to avoid any place she might be spotted by someone she knew, or worse, identified from a nearby security video. At the post office, she addressed labels to her brothers, one in care of an APO address—when someone was in the military, you weren't allowed to know their location—and one in care of the juvenile facility. She sent chocolates and souvenirs to her Grandma Adele and Grandpa Cournos, paid for shipping boxes, and sent them off.

She saw him through the door. Her breath caught. Shane Cooper, tall and beautiful as ever, was leaning back against the marble counter, exactly where he said he'd be. He wore a pulled-down baseball cap, an NYU T-shirt, jeans, and scuffed Converse high-tops. He was right on time, and Alexis beamed. A guy she could count on. Unlike Liam, she caught herself thinking uncharitably.

`I can't wait to hang out!` Shane had texted her that morning. But what did "hang out" mean to him, she wondered. Would they spend the evening just talking some more, getting to know each other, comparing stories? There was a lot, she rationalized, he could teach her about modeling, about this world. He had contacts.

But was he interested in her beyond model-talk? And if so, which Alexis should she let him see? The free-spirited, confident model-to-be, here for the summer on her way to a splashy, exciting new life? Or the scared kid from Hamtramck with a shady past and an uncertain future? The model-cute boy-magnet, or the girl who'd never had a real boyfriend before?

Alexis took a deep breath, and walked into the Max Brenner restaurant.

Chapter Fifteen
Cheat Sheet

"Grab some breakfast, and please take your seats!" Victoria clapped her hands, her chunky bamboo bangles sliding down her wiry arms. "I've called you together to go over final instructions, details, and reminders before we go into our first challenge."

Shiva-Rose ladled cut-up fruit onto her plate, snatched a croissant, and took a seat between Alexis and Lindsay. Chloe was nowhere in sight.

Victoria had set up a breakfast buffet in their photo class to prep the forty student-models for the upcoming challenge. That the first competition was near seemed impossible to Shiva-Rose.

"We're going to start by reviewing how Saturday's challenge will work, and how it will lead into future challenges," Victoria told them. "On Saturday, Mack Scarborough will give you an assignment, a specific pose to enact. You'll have time for wardrobe, makeup application, and hairstyling, and have a choice of props to help your interpretation. He will photograph each one of you individually, and then with your group. Our panel, consisting of myself and your teachers — Dan'yel, Anabelle, La Aura, and Mack — will choose your best shot, and score you individually. Then, we'll pick the best of your group shots, and you'll get an individual score for that."

"Note," complained Lindsay under her breath, "we won't have *professional* stylists, it'll be DIY. Which is really unfair."

"They expect us to use what we learned in class," Shiva-Rose responded in a whisper. "That's the point."

Lindsay rolled her eyes. She obviously considered Shiva-Rose a total know-nothing, and certainly no competition. Privately, Shiva-Rose agreed with her. Except, as Lindsay would no doubt soon point out, Shiva-Rose had a distinct advantage in this particular challenge: the "connection" the photographer had made with her.

Nothing had changed since their not-a-date last weekend. In class, behind the lens, Mack heaped praise on her dreamy expression and her penetrating eyes, but he never did or said anything inappropriate. Still, his attention was enough to make Shiva-Rose feel self-conscious.

Shiva-Rose admitted it—to herself. She wanted to win. Especially since it was going to take a miracle for her to ace the final challenge, August's fashion show runway competition. Shiva-Rose's problems with La Aura had only intensified. In class, Shiva-Rose could do nothing to earn the praise of that woman. The designer harped on Shiva-Rose's lack of style, her posture, and said that she never looked comfortable in the fashions she modeled, especially those created by La Aura herself. Her daily default criticism: "You don't convince the audience that you love what you're wearing!"

"Maybe because the clothes suck?" Lindsay would always whisper.

Now, Victoria continued to address them.

"This Saturday," she declared dramatically, "the ten girls with the lowest scores will be asked to leave school." She paused, allowing the weight of her statement to sink in. Whispers raced through the room.

"For those ten girls, whoever they turn out to be, please understand that being asked to leave is not a recrimination or personal failure. You got in to Top Model Prep because we saw something special in you, potential. A low score means only that you're not ready to continue studies. Or possibly," she emphasized with a casual shrug, "the world of modeling is not for you. In either case, it's not a bad thing."

Really? Shiva-Rose was dubious. If you flunked out this early in the competition, modeling was probably *not* in your future. Which, for this group of hopefuls, was very much a bad thing. Many had counted on this, had no plan B. Like Lindsay. And Alexis.

"On a happier note, let's talk about the girl with the highest score," Victoria switched into chirpy mode. "One of you will have to accrue a score of A-plus or A in both your solo shot and performance in your group portrait. That girl will be declared winner of our first challenge. She'll receive incredible prizes and go into the next challenges with a huge advantage: immunity. She cannot be eliminated in the second session, no matter how low her scores.

"Here's the best tip I can give you," Victoria concluded. "Focus on the big picture. Every challenge you make it through is one step closer to the final runway fashion show, where the ten girls left will model La Aura's exclusive new line. That's what you want to be thinking about. Our big winner will be one of those ten—and handed the keys to a fabulous future!"

"That's so unfair!" Lindsay groused as Victoria departed and Mack sauntered into the classroom, his mere presence bringing heat to Shiva-Rose's cheeks. "Our futures depend on the worst designer in town? Seriously, who can make her stuff look good?"

Shiva-Rose and Alexis looked over their shoulders.

"Aside from *her*!" Lindsay huffed, following their gaze.

Chloe had taken a seat behind them, eyes glued to her iPhone. She didn't look up.

"La Aura is so kissing up to her," Lindsay whispered. "She totally thinks Chloe Huntley can make her clothes famous."

"She probably can," Alexis said with a shrug.

"It's business," Shiva-Rose commented. "If Chloe Huntley wins, it's a win for La Aura, too.

Lots of publicity, maybe she'll design a mother-daughter ensemble for the cover of *Vogue*."

"We'll see," Lindsay muttered, unamused.

"But La Aura isn't the only judge," Alexis pointed out. "You have to get high marks from Dan'yel, Anabelle, Mack. And Victoria—who hasn't seemed all that chummy with Chloe lately."

"True," Lindsay mused with a mischievous glint in her eyes. "Aunt Vickie is still in shock over Chloe's meltdown last week. But speaking of big fans, yours is on the judging panel, too," Lindsay said to Shiva-Rose. "I bet he'll do whatever he can to up your grade, assuming he gets your cooperation. Leading him on is a good career move."

"I want to succeed on my own merit," Shiva-Rose said defensively.

"Ladies? Everything okay over here?" Mack himself interrupted their conversation, striding over and making Shiva-Rose's heart leap.

"Peachy." Alexis grinned, tossing her red curls over one shoulder.

Mack's brow furrowed. "Actually, Alexis, I've been meaning to talk to you about something that concerns me," he said.

Shiva-Rose was glad Mack wasn't singling her out, but she felt a pang of concern for her roommate. Shiva-Rose wondered if Mack, like her, suspected something was off with Alexis lately.

Mack, in full instructor mode now, and acting way older than his eighteen years, leaned over and tilted Alexis's chin toward him. Shiva-Rose couldn't help the jolt of jealousy that went through her.

"A model's best asset is her eyes," Mack explained, frowning. "Yours have been bleary and red lately. And what's this puffiness and dark circles underneath them?"

Alexis shrugged.

"Too much partying is not cool," he admonished her. "Not now. When the competition's over, there'll be plenty of time."

Lindsay perked up. Clearly, this was news to her.

Shiva-Rose had to say something—even a lie.

"What are you implying?" She jumped in, feeling protective. "She's not party—"

But Mack just shook his head, turned on his heel, and went to grab his cameras. "Group 14A," he said, all business now, "you're up first."

Shiva-Rose sighed. Alexis was out every night now, returning later and later each time. She was beautiful, but at some point, burning the candle at both ends had to show on her face. It wasn't surprising that a photographer looking through an unforgiving lens would notice it first. But how long before the others did? Victoria, Dan'yel, Anabelle?

What *was* Alexis doing every night? Shiva-Rose suspected shoplifting, but hoped her little lecture had had some effect on the girl. And she was probably also spending time with that underwear model, Shane. But . . . every night? Alexis was flirting with danger.

"Shiva-Rose." Mack's touch on her shoulder was light. Still, she jumped just a little. Class had ended, and the girls were filing out. "Hang on."

"Um, I have to—"

"I developed the pictures from the ferry." His eyes sparkled. "Of you."

She swallowed, unsure what the right reaction was.

"They're pretty amazing," he said tenderly, "I'd like to show them to you."

I bet you would, she heard Lindsay's voice singsong in her head. How annoying.

"How about we grab a bite tomorrow night, and I'll bring them?"

Grab a bite. Tomorrow night. She parsed his words as though they needed interpretation. Mack Scarborough was asking her out.

"I don't think that's a good idea," Shiva-Rose said levelly. It hit her just then, a careening realization. She'd said the exact same thing to him last Saturday before they went on the ferry. But he'd talked her into going with him then—and she knew, in the way a girl sometimes knows these things, he would again.

"It's just a neighborhood dive," Mack explained, his hand on the small of her back as he led Shiva-Rose into Food, a grungy diner squeezed onto a miniscule triangle of street.

"Right," she laughed. This was the kind of "dive"—tiny, crowded, dark, beat-up—so downmarket it was up-market. Shiva-Rose remembered reading a gossip magazine that had mentioned Food. Only the hippest, New York-iest celebrities went there, the kind who didn't want to be noticed.

Like Leo DiCaprio, with a baseball cap so far down his face all you saw was chin and brim, or Hollywood starlets like Evan Rachel Wood and the cast from *Nick and Norah's Infinite Playlist*.

"Hey, Mackie." A tat-sleeved waitress gestured to a small, candlelit table in a corner. "Nice to see you again."

And very hip fashion photographers, Shiva-Rose thought, with a smile. Obviously they came here, too.

As they threaded their way through the joint, Mack nodded at a few other diners. Was he trying to impress her?

"So, Mack daddy," said a scruffy-bearded waiter once they were seated, with a nod toward Shiva-Rose, "I see you brought a friend today. Obviously a model. Your protégée?"

Or . . . was he trying to impress others?

Either way, Shiva-Rose felt flattered, glad she'd chosen a shoulder-baring halter top in burnt orange, her best color.

Mack played it very cool, very gentlemanly. He introduced Shiva-Rose as one of the students from Top Model Prep, and then ordered them both Diet Cokes and a margarita pizza to share. True to his word, and in spite of the tight quarters, Mack did show her the photos he'd taken on the Staten Island Ferry. He had not overstated how amazing they'd come out. Shiva-Rose barely recognized herself as that girl with the faraway look in her eyes.

"What are you going to do with them?" Shiva-Rose asked, digging into the most delicious pizza she'd ever eaten.

"Use them in my portfolio, for sure," Mack replied. "Unless you have some objection to that."

Should she? Was it against Top Model's rules? Mack read her hesitation. "Of course, I'm not going to show them to anyone until after the competition. For now, these are just between the two of us. Our secret."

Shiva-Rose stopped midbite. Another secret he was sharing with her alone. Doubt nudged her hard. What was he doing? Playing her? Or was it the other way around?

Lindsay's voice was in her ear: *Flirt with him, why don't you? Lead him on.*

Shiva-Rose had never in her life led on a boy. It wasn't her style. And woe to the guy who led her on! *Calm down*, she ordered herself. What about the possibility that no one was playing anyone? That they were just two people who enjoyed hanging out with each other? So what if Mack had entrusted her not to tell that he'd lied about his age to Top Model Prep? And so what, if after the competition ended, he used her photos in his portfolio? They were great shots, and could only help her own career.

And she reassured herself that tonight, even if it felt more like a date, was one hundred percent innocent. Kosher.

"Nervous about Sunday?" Mack asked, finishing off his soda.

"A little," she admitted. "I would die if I got eliminated."

"Not gonna happen," Mack assured her. "I can give you a little inside info — if you want." He leaned in toward her, so close their faces were almost touching. "If you knew now what the theme of the photo shoot was going to be — what I'll be having you pose as — it'd be a little heads-up. Because there's going to be a twist to the competition that no one knows about."

Shiva-Rose held her breath.

He slid his hand across the tiny table and intertwined their fingers. Mack's voice was low, raspy, irresistible. "I'll give you a cheat sheet—if you promise not to tell."

Chapter Sixteen
Meltdown

Thunderstorms had been predicted. Chloe sank down against the rooftop guardrail, hoping the skies would open soon. She wanted to get caught in the kind of drenching rain LA only rarely got, the kind that soaked through to your bones and sent the mascara running down your face.

She wanted her face to reflect her feelings, the opposite of everything she'd ever been taught by her mom.

As the first drops began to fall, she took out her iPhone to read the texts again. To let the horror sink in.

Over the past few days, she'd patched things up with Liam. They were trading texts again and had talked a couple of times, and she had started to forgive him. Even if she still didn't understand why he'd so readily believed the bogus message barring him from visiting her. Why had he agreed that she was a spoiled brat who held herself above the rules, and gone so far as to say, "If it were true, how would it look for me—Senator Lattimore's son—to be breaking your school's rules? We always have to think about that, Chloe. You know it?"

But it hadn't been true, Chloe had argued back. He wouldn't have been breaking or bending any rules by coming.

Chloe knew now that Victoria had never called Liam. The damage-doer had to be Charlotte. Chloe's mother's hand was all over this deception, no matter how vehemently she denied it.

"Liam is a distraction." She'd said that. It followed that Charlotte would do anything to keep them apart. Even lie about Top Model's rules, tell him to ignore whatever Chloe said to the contrary.

But Liam had finally won her over when he'd sent her flowers. Two dozen long-stemmed roses. And the cutest stuffed bear on a surfboard, with a note that read I'LL CATCH THE NEXT WAVE OUT.

But now all the warmth and fuzziness Chloe felt toward Liam came crashing down. The boy was a liar.

A cheater.

Chloe had been in photo class when her phone began buzzing nonstop with a blizzard of messages. She'd scooted out early to call people back, to try and understand what she was reading, She must've sent dozens of e-mails and texts, made a bunch of calls. All except the one she was too scared to make.

Now, she clicked on the icon for messages. They were all still there.

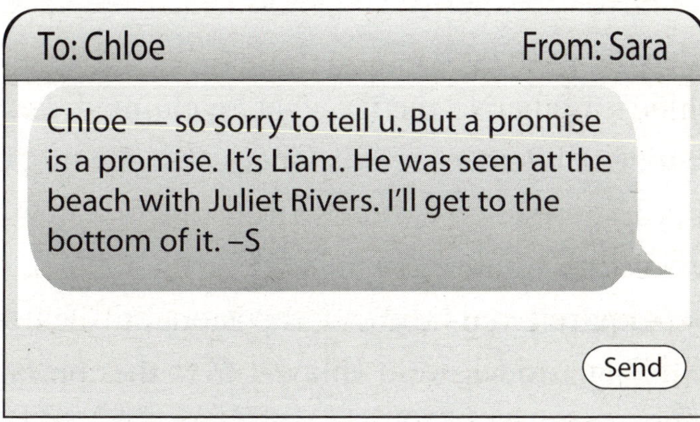

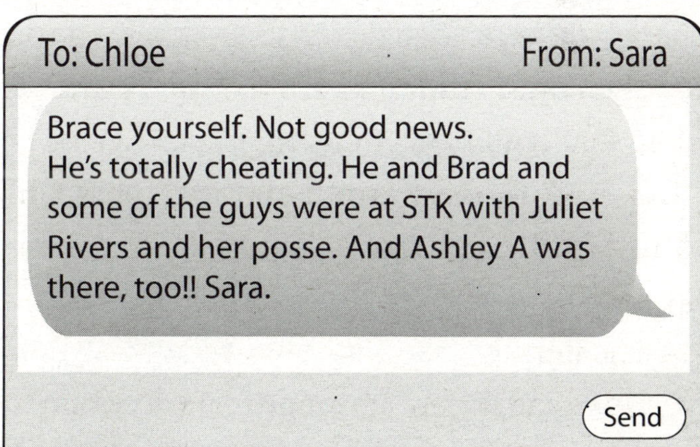

Other friends had sent photos. Liam—trying to duck his head, but definitely him—among Juliet's posse, coming out of a club. In another, Liam was holding hands with the pouty-lipped starlet.

The messages, back and forth, and the calls, continued into the night. No one had actually spoken to Liam. But he hadn't gone out of his way to call anyone, either.

So it had to be true.

As did this: No matter what he claimed, Liam didn't care that Chloe was lonely, that she missed him. Liam had elsewhere to be, someone new to be with.

Chloe felt as if she'd been lacerated. Gutted. As if her insides were splayed over this rooftop floor.

To: Chloe From: Sara

U need to come back now.
Confront him.

Send

A new message came in. From Sara.

Right—like that was easy! Chloe couldn't just charter a jet, or even fly commercial and bop out to the West Coast. Sure, if she took Sara's advice, there was still a chance. She could quit the competition, regain her freedom and, hopefully, her boyfriend.

But standing in the way was the obstacle Chloe had never been able to overcome: her own mother. The wrath of Charlotte Huntley was legendary, and for good reason. When crossed, Charlotte's game was the cold shoulder. And once iced by Charlotte, no one successfully crawled back into her good graces. You'd never see that smile again, or be wrapped in that warm hug. Just ask Chloe's stepbrother, or her own father, for that matter.

Chloe put her head on her knees, and as the rain fell, she let the tears come.

Chapter Seventeen
The Photo Shoot

Lindsay felt the first beads of sweat forming on her forehead and could only pray it wouldn't get much worse.

"Tell me again *why* we're doing this outside when it's hot enough to melt tires?" she groaned as the students gathered on Top Model Prep's rooftop garden Saturday morning.

"You know why. Mack Scarborough thinks everyone looks best in natural light," Alexis replied.

"Nice of them to keep *that* little detail under wraps until the last minute," Lindsay huffed, glancing at Shiva-Rose, who seemed totally distracted.

"It's hot, but look." Alexis pointed upward. The sky was blanketed in gray. "No direct sunlight is optimum for photos. I think it's cool."

She thinks everything is cool. Lindsay made a face at her.

"Welcome, my ladies," said Victoria, looking extrachic this steamy morning, not a wrinkle on her face or on her sleek white pantsuit. "Today is your most important day so far. This is what you've been waiting for"—she paused for dramatic effect—"your first challenge, Top Model Prep's photo shoot."

A wave of excitement rippled through the crowd, accompanied by nervous high-pitched chatter. Everyone knew the stakes: Do well, and stay on. Do poorly, and don't let the door hit you on the butt.

"Try not to freak out," Dan'yel, still panting from schlepping up the one flight of stairs to the rooftop, clarified. "You'll all do fantastically. How could you not? You're great beauties, we've taught you well, and Mack Scarborough knows how to get the best shots out of you."

Lindsay politely applauded along with the rest. But she had no illusions. Photo-boy: Not a close personal friend. He would not be working hard to coax the best shot out of *her.* He had an eye, and gentle guidance, only for one of them.

But Shiva-Rose clearly had something else on her mind. "Where's Chloe?" she asked, looking around nervously. "She promised not to be late."

"Maybe she changed her mind, doesn't care anymore," Lindsay said with a smirk.

Chloe had been a complete mess since the onslaught of texts yesterday. She'd hidden in her room all morning, resisted Shiva-Rose's and Alexis's entrees of empathy. All Lindsay could think was, *welcome to real competition*. That was what her roommates didn't understand.

That's why, no matter what, they could never really be friends.

Mack cleared his throat, drawing the students' attention to him.

"Since this is the first competition and I know everyone's nerves are a little jangly, we'll follow the exact format we use in our class exercises. You all remember, right?"

Could he be any more condescending? Lindsay thought, irritated.

"Each group will be assigned a theme, and each model, a specific role within it. Today, you'll be coached by either Dan'yel, Anabelle, La Aura, or Victoria. I know we'd told you the makeup would be DIY, but here's a twist: You'll also have the option of using professional hairdressers and makeup artists. Because . . . we're mixing it up a little." He paused for dramatic effect. "Each group will be posing not just for the challenge, but also for a real client."

"A theme and a client? I don't get it." Bikini spoke for most of them.

"For example," Mack explained. "Remember when the theme was flowers? And Shiva-Rose was a calla lily?" Shiva-Rose's jaw clenched. "Say we did that same theme today, only you'd have a client, the famous jeweler, Tiffany. Our lovely calla lily might use a delicate gold chain to spruce up her look. A creative melding of theme and client. Got it? And don't worry," Mack assured them, "you'll have a friendly coach to help."

Victoria had exciting news for them. "As an extra added bonus, the group with the combined best score will get to pose in a *real ad campaign* for their client. So, even if you're not the challenge winner, your entire group could get a huge boost. How do you like that?"

Judging by the squeal-enhanced applause, the models very much liked it.

"It's all good," Anabelle put in as Mack got ready to assign themes and clients to the groups.

The girls across the hall in 14A learned they'd be posing for Waves, a retailer for activewear. Their theme was the beach. Ava, Jana, Faye, and, yep, Bikini would model bathing suits. Anabelle was their coach.

The model-hopefuls from suite 15D scored Hanes as a client and La Aura as a coach. They were to be a soccer team, modeling athletic-wear.

Other groups' clients were companies famous for jewelry, handbags, bikes, and designer jeans. Themes included "red carpet," "horror film cast," "eco-protesters," and "circus performers."

"Rock 'n' roll!" Mack did an air guitar pose, acting like he'd saved the best for Lindsay and her group. "Your theme is rock band. Your client is Kitson, specifically their sneakers and shoes. Your mission is to create rocker poses that show off funky footwear. Pretty cool, huh?"

"I'm so about music and shoes!" Alexis raved.

"Hang on." Mack shaded his eyes and looked around. "Why am I only counting three of you? Where's Chloe?"

"I think she's still in her room. I'll go get her," Shiva-Rose said, hurrying off.

• • •

The shoot was outdoors, but the girls would get ready in the big dressing room off the photo studio. Even Lindsay admitted to serious awe as she took in the care and planning Top Model Prep had put into the setup.

The dressing room was crammed with fabulous fashions chosen to represent the clients and themes. Lindsay passed by surfboards, soccer balls, cleats, sparkly jewelry, the latest handbags, even a Ducati motorcycle for the lucky girls in 12F, who'd be posing for a bike retailer. And finally seeing her beloved makeup artists, hairstylists, and assistants actually made her tingle. They were a vestige of her former life as a star when she was waited on hand and foot, and a little reminder of what this, all her scheming, planning, dreaming, was all about.

She and Alexis came to a stop before the musical instruments that were set aside for 14C. Shiva-Rose was still off collecting Chloe.

"Ticktock." Dan'yel tapped his watch. "Timing counts in the challenge."

Lindsay designated herself lead singer, while Alexis had dibs on percussion, and immediately began playing the drums. Lindsay wondered why Shiva-Rose and Chloe hadn't returned yet.

An unfamiliar feeling skittered inside her. What if Chloe somehow had figured out it was her behind the phony letter to Liam? That it was Lindsay who'd planted the rumors, set them in motion? What if Chloe was not in her room, sobbing uncontrollably, but coolly compiling evidence against her? A sudden wave of nausea threatened Lindsay's confidence.

"Lindsay, your role needs explaining, but—" Dan'yel began.

"I'm lead singer, of course," she interjected.

"One of two . . ."

Lindsay's eyebrow shot up. She and Chloe were coleads? Whose idea was that? Unless the girl didn't show, that is . . .

"Oh, Chloe! *There* you are, darling. Perfect timing. I was just telling Lindsay that Mack and I think it would make an amazing shot if the two of you portrayed lead singers with *wildly* different styles. Lindsay, you're the pop star, the teen idol."

Lindsay wasn't listening. She was still processing Chloe, who looked like her kitten just died.

She was even paler than usual, fragile seeming, her eyes puffy and red. They were going to need a ton of makeup to cover her up.

Lindsay was hugely relieved.

Until Dan'yel declared, "And you, Chloe, will be the band's goth girl."

Black eyeliner, black eye shadow, tattered soul. Chloe's dark mood would actually work *for* her.

Whatever borderline remorse Lindsay had felt about her prank vanished.

"That's it!" Mack said as Shiva-Rose posed for her solo shots. "Lower the guitar . . . that's right . . . down by your hips!"

While the girls had been getting ready, backdrops and tripods had been set up on the roof, along with umbrellas to bounce the natural light. A soundtrack ripped through the humid air, blasting guitar riffs.

Shiva-Rose was poured into black liquid leggings and a sequined bustier. She looked amazing, but, to Lindsay, didn't seem that into channeling a fierce rock goddess. Something had clearly happened between Shiva-Rose and Mack. Now, in front of his camera, she wasn't herself.

Mack kept coaxing her, pushing her to go further. "You're da bomb, Shiva-Rose. Give me attitude!"

Da bomb. Lindsay rolled her eyes. Couldn't they have idiotproofed the challenge?

"Remember to *breathe*. Your only obligation in life is to breathe." Anabelle swooped in from the sidelines with a nonsensical yoga cliché.

"Let's see those shiny red patent leather diva heels—remember your client," pragmatic Victoria called out.

"Shift your weight between your hips," Dan'yel directed.

In attempting to follow every direction thrown at her, Shiva-Rose pretzeled her body like she was trapped in a game of Twister.

"Be a bold one!" Alexis urged.

"She's not doing a detergent commercial." Lindsay, sworn not to help anyone, couldn't restrain herself. "Stop posing, Shiva-Rose. Let's see your ferocious concentration. Your focus. That's what you're good at."

Direction by Lindsay seemed to kick-start Shiva-Rose. It was almost as if she'd suddenly come out of a trance.

She used her kohl-rimmed, glittery eyes to signal a shift in mood. She did one pose staring at her instrument. In another, she bit her lip and looked skyward. In a third, she hugged her guitar to her chest and kicked one leg in the air. The photos were going to kill.

Lindsay didn't know whether to feel proud or peeved.

Alexis was brilliant. The idea to topknot her hair using actual wood drumsticks was genius. That, and her Amy Winehouse–winged eyeliner, said, "Don't mess with me." Clad in a leather dress and long ropes of gold beads, she was all energy, pounding away, working up a sweat as a real rock drummer would.

Mack clicked away happily. Mindful of her client, Alexis did some standing poses, leaning against the drums and sticking her feet out. The snakeskin ankle strap heels caught the light of the flash. Lindsay couldn't help but be impressed. Who knew that the naïve Midwestern girl, regardless of whatever strange secrets she had, could be such a pro?

The hairdressers had fitted Chloe in a black spiky wig. The inky color was shocking against her extrapale skin. She was wearing a fishnet top with a lace cami underneath, a low-slung studded belt, and denim cutoffs. High-heeled gladiator sandals with leather straps twisted up her calf. She wore thick charcoal liner above and below each eyelid, spider eyelashes, and, in a stroke of goth genius, white lipstick. Chloe had done more than mere "pretty in punk." She'd pulled off dirtbag chic.

In one pose, she glowered at the camera. In another, she sulked. For the bonus round, she actually used the acoustic guitar and smashed it over her knee, her face twisted in pain. Beneath all that makeup, her poses were painfully raw and real. Chloe's photos were going to show a girl vacillating between devastation and fury.

And Lindsay wasn't going to get one ounce of credit for it. How much did that suck?

Lindsay admittedly was not in optimum headspace for her own solo shots. But that wasn't the reason for the disaster.

It had started in the dressing room.

She'd been so excited to have professional stylists and assistants there. Only when they started working with her, Lindsay balked at everything—her outfit, her shoes, the hairstylist's ideas. She was supposed to be playing a pop star—secretly, she'd chosen Katy Perry to base her character on. Beyoncé if she *had* to, but that look was so played.

Lindsay envisioned a micro-miniskirt, stiletto boots, and silk blouse. Instead, the stylists insisted on PVC leggings, a distressed dress, and suede tasseled ankle boots. They'd wanted her hair in some dippy flip. She lobbied for an extreme 'fro: wild, frizzy, out-there. The compromise was tousled waves, extensions, and a sequined headband. The one thing everyone agreed on was a shrunken leather jacket.

Finally ready for her close-up, Lindsay treated the microphone cord like a feather boa, wrapping it around her shoulders, then kissing it coquettishly. She was belting "I Kissed a Girl" along with Katy over the speakers.

Victoria abruptly killed the music. "It's about the *shoes*, Lindsay, not just you," she pointed out sharply.

Miffed, Lindsay complied. She lay down on her back, and supported by her arms, started pedaling her legs. An upside-down bicycle exercise, starring stupid shoes — if that's what they wanted, that's what they'd get!

Sweating profusely now, she asked for a makeup refresh and a bottle of water. Then, she stood up, threw her hair back, and held the mic away from her, as if she was screaming the lyrics.

"Here, take a guitar and give me Taylor Swift," Mack told her.

Unthrilled with such curt direction, still, Lindsay channeled what she knew. She gripped the guitar with one hand, leaned into it — and this should have been recognized for the total genius it was — made herself cry.

"What are you doing?" Mack looked up from his camera. "There's no crying in rock 'n' roll."

"Oh, snap," said Lindsay, her voice laced with sarcasm. "But you're referencing a movie as old as my grandma. I'm doing Taylor Swift. 'Teardrops On My Guitar'? Her first number one song?"

Sniping at the photographer. Not the best way to gain points or respect here. But Mack wasn't even trying to understand her. She, a card-carrying actress, knew exactly what she was doing.

"Let's do another pose," Dan'yel gently suggested. "Lose the guitar, get the mic again. Go back to being lead singer."

Lindsay faced the camera. She twirled the mic as if it were a weapon.

"Back straight and shoulders up," Anabelle again demonstrated. "You must never forget to feed your heart chakra."

Lindsay paid no attention to Anabelle's non sequitur, but what came next from Mack's curled lip stopped her cold and sent her reeling back to age thirteen. "You're slouching. Slouching makes you look fat."

The remark landed like a slap across the face, bringing the sting of real tears. And then she seethed. No one called Lindsay Robinson fat. 'Cause she'd been there. She'd been to that being-ashamed-of-herself place. And she'd sworn to never go back there again.

And now this. One crack from moron-boy with a camera, and Lindsay was right back *there*, fighting shame and tears of rage.

At the camera's next click, she scowled bitterly.

Not so much the sunny pop star.

• • •

Then came the time to shoot the band.

Mack instructed the models to ditch the instruments. "The group shot has to be about relationships within a group. You all need to be of a piece, each individual strengthening the whole."

Lindsay exchanged a concerned look with her roommates, which Dan'yel mistook for confusion.

"It's as if solo artists like Adele, Duffy, Leona Lewis, even Miley, are together in a supergroup!" he piped up.

Dan'yel's attempt at hip amused Lindsay, who'd gotten over her stupid crying jag and pulled herself together. "We got it, Dad, no worries."

"And don't forget—" Dan'yel said.

"The shoes," Alexis, Lindsay, and Shiva-Rose chorused.

Dan'yel smiled. "Go to it. I want to see you rock this. I want to see you win."

Mack had them stand next to each other, which felt like a perp lineup to Lindsay. But she didn't blurt her sentiment out loud. He asked for hands on hips, arms at their sides, then for Shiva-Rose and Lindsay, the tallest, to angle themselves as if they were bracketing Chloe and Alexis. Lindsay dutifully obeyed every instruction even though, in her view, every setup managed to favor Shiva-Rose.

But she had to keep it together and hope Mack wouldn't hold a grudge for that little episode during the solo session. Her mouth had gotten the best of her then, but she was determined to keep it cool and professional for the second half.

If only Mack hadn't insisted, "Lindsay, Shiva-Rose, and Alexis, I want you three to form a semicircle behind Chloe."

"Like she's the star and we're the backup singers?" It came out before Lindsay could self-censor.

Dan'yel flashed his eyes at her, a warning.

Chloe slid her eyes over to Lindsay, and gave her smug smile. She took a step forward, in front of the others.

No one said a word.

Lindsay had no choice but to follow suit and grin and bear it as Mack snapped the shot.

"For the last take, here's what I want." Mack described, "a really tight and together, girl-band, girl-power shot. Shiva-Rose and Alexis, take far right and far left. Chloe and Lindsay in the middle, arms around each other."

"I'm not comfortable with that," Chloe said immediately.

"Not happening," Lindsay chimed in.

"It's not your choice," Dan'yel reminded them. "This is professional time. You do what the photographer tells you."

Awkwardly, they did as instructed, but Lindsay jutted her head forward a tad and smiled dazzlingly.

"You're overplaying it," Chloe said through gritted teeth. "This is not like being onstage and playing to the last row in the audience. Photography is more intimate. You can get more across with subtlety. Do a slight wink or a half curve of the lip. Tip your head away from me."

"How about I just turn all the way away from you?" Lindsay retorted.

She did exactly that.

Chloe reacted in kind.

"If that's the way you girls want to play it," Mack said, giving up. And that was the shot. Chloe and Lindsay, back-to-back, arms crossed defensively.

No way they'll choose that image to grade us on. That was Lindsay's last thought before Mack called it a wrap.

Chapter Eighteen
And the Winner Is . . .

The panel, Victoria, Anabelle, Dan'yel, Mack, and La Aura, were in their seats. They'd taken what seemed like an eternity to judge the photos, determine the scores, and now, finally, deliver the results.

The wait, only two and a half hours in reality, had been excruciating. Lindsay spent the entire time in the gym, Chloe had texted her friends, and Shiva-Rose tried in vain to teach Alexis how to play poker.

"I just don't have the gambling gene," Alexis said, mistakenly tossing away a winning hand.

"You gamble every day," Shiva-Rose admonished Alexis. "With your entire future."

Let's not go there, Alexis thought. Shiva-Rose had a moral streak a mile wide, but in light of recent events, Alexis could no longer condemn her for it.

At just past seven P.M., forty girls got identical texts from Victoria: **`Meet me in the photo studio at 7:30.`**

I should be nervous. Alexis knew it, but for some reason, she wasn't. She looked around at her peers filing into the room, taking seats. Nervous buzzy energy filled the air. Some girls clutched talismans, Alexis noted a few praying, and nearly everyone, except Lindsay and Chloe, was holding hands. They were about to find out which group had won over their client, who dazzled the judges and won the challenge, and which ten were going home tonight.

Alexis glanced over at Lindsay, who radiated cool, calm, supreme confidence. The girl was either a wonderful actress, or in complete denial.

Does she even know how much she sabotaged herself?

Without her usual welcoming preamble, Victoria cut to the chase. "We graded you realistically, not as students in class, but as if you were professionals pitching your client. So if it sounds like we were harsh, I'm sorry, but—"

"Welcome to the real world of modeling, kiddies," Mack cracked. "You might as well learn it now."

Oh, we learned, Alexis mused, *more than you ever meant to teach us.*

"We took your solo shot and your group shot into consideration. Did you stand out in the group shot? What did it say to us?" Anabelle scanned the room as if waiting for a response.

"More important," La Aura inserted, "did you do your job, showcase the client's product? Their representatives were the final judges of that." She nodded to the group seated just behind the panel.

"The girls from suite 14A, we'll start with you," Victoria said, smiling so genuinely Alexis could see the crinkles at her eyes. "Please come to the front of the room."

Faye, Ava, Bikini, and Jana nervously rose and approached the panel. Alexis leaned over to squeeze Faye's hand. Shiva-Rose wished them good luck.

"Your theme was the beach," Victoria said to the quivering quartet in front of her. "You posed in beachwear for your client, Waves. Let's see how you did."

The big-screen monitor behind the judges filled with their images. Alexis was no longer a fan of Mack Scarborough the person, but as a photographer? Instantly, she saw why he'd gotten the gig as Top Model's in-house prodigy. He'd taken four pretty-but-unpolished girls, and through the camera's eye, turned them into professional models.

"We'll start with the solo shots," Victoria said. "Ava, you're up first."

The screen filled with an image of dark-skinned Ava, who rocked her bikini, and did an adorable pose peeking out from behind her surfboard. Surely an A, if Alexis were to judge. The panel did not agree.

"You were cute," Victoria explained, "but you did not exude confidence. Instead, you came off tentative. No one would believe you're a real surfer."

Ava got a grade of B. She was thrilled. It meant she probably wasn't going home.

Faye did not fare so well posing on a skateboard. "We tried to pick your best shot," Mack told her, "but take after take, your body language screamed, 'Help! Get me off this!'"

It was true. Faye was smiling bravely, but up on the big screen, you couldn't miss the fear in her eyes.

"You should have gotten off the skateboard," Victoria advised. "Found a more comfortable pose. You need to think more creatively."

Faye was clearly bummed about her grade, a C.

Contrary to name-allusion expectations, Bikini just messed up. She pouted when she should have laughed, tensed when she should have been breezy. She tried to play up her string-bikini-worthy curves, but lost points for obscuring the boogie board.

She had to settle for a C-.

Jana was the strongest of the group, and not just because her pencil-thin body did wonders for the boy shorts and crop top she modeled. Her best shot was her flip-wheelie. With her right foot, she'd pushed down on the curved tip of the board, flipped it in the air, and caught it in her left hand. The entire room applauded. Jana sashayed away with an A.

Reviews for 14A's group shot were similarly mixed. The representative from Waves was complimentary, but not hugely impressed. She wasn't going to hire them for an ad.

Other groups were called before 14Cs, and many As were awarded, but Alexis continued to feel good about their chances. Until they were called. That's when a clutch of nerves grabbed Alexis by the throat, threatening to choke her.

"Breathe," Shiva-Rose whispered, mimicking crazy Anabelle. "Your only responsibility in life is to breathe."

Alexis laughed in spite of herself.

"I'm glad you're in a cheerful mood, Alexis, because we've got some good news for you," Victoria chirped. "Here's your solo shot."

Mack had caught her drumming up a storm, chin up, topknot askew, foot bouncing on the drum pedal. That was the kicker. He'd managed to get a shot that made her look like a real rocker. But those snakeskin ankle strap heels nearly stole center stage!

"That pose is pure invention!" marveled Dan'yel. "If I didn't know better, I'd believe you were in a band."

"If I wanted to be a rock drummer, I'd run out and get that footwear." Their client, the Kitson rep, beamed. "I love your pose, Alexis."

"Alexis, I'm thrilled to tell you, your solo shot earns you an A!" Victoria delivered the amazing news.

A wave of intense joy shot through her. *They love my pose! They love my pose!* Alexis danced on the spot as Shiva-Rose hugged her. *Whoo-hoo!*

Shiva-Rose was called next. Her best shot, as it turned out, was the one where Lindsay had coached her. She looked so caught up in the music, she appeared unaware of the camera. Shiva-Rose got a strong A-.

If Mack's favorite was surprised that Alexis had outdone her, she didn't show it. If anything, Shiva-Rose looked positively gleeful that she hadn't gotten the top grade.

And then there was Lindsay. Alexis had been right to worry. The former child star had been so mouthy, so sarcastic, such a show-off in her photos and her 'tude. She got called out for all of it. Luckily, the photo they picked to judge her on was snapped after she deigned to take direction from Mack and Dan'yel. The upside-down, legs-in-the-air bicycle shot probably saved her from a certain failing grade. She got a B.

Unhappy, Lindsay tried to stomp away, but Shiva-Rose pulled her back. "We have to hear about the group shot, you can't just leave."

Lindsay scowled. She probably didn't want to hang around to hear the kudos undoubtedly coming Chloe's way.

Victoria *was* totally gushing. "Chloe does goth! Who knew you had it in you, the sunny California girl!"

"Does your mama know you can play against type?" Dan'yel jested. "Or do I get to tell her?"

Anabelle found Chloe's stormy eyes a "key to her soul."

Victoria awarded Chloe "our highest grade, an A-plus."

Channeling Lindsay, Alexis couldn't help but think *of course*. But she couldn't dwell too much, because the panel was moving on to the group shot. The image they called up was the final one Mack had shot, with Chloe and Lindsay standing back-to-back.

A disaster when they were shooting it, Alexis had to admit the image looked kinda cool up there on the big screen.

"Alexis," Dan'yel began, "Let's start with you."

Alexis studied herself. She'd been smart, she realized, to ignore the drama and focus on her own pose. She'd played the cute card. She'd swiveled her hip out and brought two fingers to her forehead for an endearing military salute. She'd drawn attention to her electric eyes and got the love.

"Even though you're the smallest, and stuck behind Chloe and Lindsay, you made that shot your own," raved Dan'yel. "I'm proud of you."

"You get an A-plus for the group shot." Victoria cheered. "Congratulations!"

Her high jump at hearing her score could have won her a gold in the Olympics. "I can't believe it!" Alexis cried. Joy flooded through her.

An A in the solos, and an A+ in the group shot. The highest marks given out so far—but that couldn't possibly be enough to win the whole challenge, right? Chloe got an A+, too. She'd have to earn another in the group shot to beat Alexis. In a fair competition, she wouldn't. Chloe had fought with Lindsay, totally messed up in the group shot. Everyone on the panel knew it.

Would she get the best score anyway, because, after all, she was Chloe Huntley?

"Shiva-Rose, you're next," Victoria called.

"What I don't understand," Dan'yel said, "is why you allowed yourself to fade into the background in the group shot? Things were chaotic between Chloe and Lindsay, but you, Shiva-Rose, got lost completely."

Alexis, concerned for her roommate, instinctively put a protective arm around Shiva-Rose's waist. Were they about to give her a bad grade?

"I'm happy to say you got high points from your client for rocking those red patent leather diva heels," Victoria told her. "That's what saved you. We're giving you a B-plus for the group shot."

The whole time Mack Scarborough said not one word about Shiva-Rose's photos.

The focus then turned to Chloe and Lindsay. The representative from Kitson was blunt in her assessment. "No one looking at this picture is going to be interested in those boots. I don't know how you did it, but you managed to take our most expensive, showiest footwear and render them invisible. Sorry, girls, I would never book you."

A collective gasp filled the room. Harsh!

"You did let your mood get in the way here," Dan'yel agreed. "Despite the photographer's specific instructions."

Victoria's comment was unexpectedly thoughtful. "It's obvious you girls are not getting along. Do you know what this photo says to me?" She looked from Chloe to Lindsay. "Maybe these two girls could be friends, or were friends once. But something happened between you. And now, whatever animosity you have toward one another is consuming you. You *can't* tell me that's what you were going for."

"That's exactly it."

"Absolutely."

Defiantly, the judges gave Chloe and Lindsay their grades.

They received the exact same one: C.

Alexis exhaled. So they weren't unfairly favoring Chloe. Maybe there was some justice in the world.

Chloe's expression, glum to begin with, remained unchanged, and she slunk off the roof garden. Lindsay's eyes flashed dangerously and she stomped off in the other direction. Neither hung around to hear which girls were leaving, and who won the challenge.

So it was left to Alexis and Shiva-Rose to console Bikini, who wound up in the bottom ten, and would be leaving that night.

And it was left to Shiva-Rose, all on her own from 14C, to scream as loud as she could, and hug as hard as she could, and to practically do CPR, because the winner of the challenge nearly passed out when she heard her name:

"Alexis Cournos!"

Chapter Nineteen
Chance of a Lifetime

"I owe it all to you!" Alexis could not, for the life of her, becalm herself since hearing her name announced as the photo shoot winner. "It's all because of you guys! You have no idea what this means to me."

Lindsay sniffed. She still couldn't believe it. Really? *Alexis?* Some kid from some . . . flyover state . . . not even tall enough to really model. How could they have given it to her?

To add insult to injury, Alexis insisted, *insisted*, on taking the whole "team" out to celebrate. She'd gotten special dispensation from the powers-that-be to break curfew (irony alert) and treat them to a late night dessert at her favorite place, Max Brenner's calorie emporium. They were instantly escorted to the best spot in the house, the "see and be seen" table.

Well, at least I *still look amazing after the awful day I had*, Lindsay thought, laying her napkin on her lap.

"I'm so happy, I could order the whole entire menu!" Alexis declared, her eyes dancing, her complexion still flushed.

"And pay for it, how?" Lindsay demanded. "You won money to shop at Barneys, I don't think you can redeem it in chocolate chunks."

"Do they pay you for being a buzzkill?" Chloe got up in Lindsay's face.

"Seriously. Just give it a rest tonight, Lindsay." Shiva-Rose sounded tired. "Can't you be happy for Alexis?"

"I'm not unhappy you won," Lindsay told Alexis unconvincingly. "I just don't see the urgent need for celebration. What did the rest of us get out of it besides humiliation?"

"Proof that I can rise to any challenge, even though my life is falling apart?" Chloe said soberly. "That's something to celebrate, I guess."

Her life is falling apart? Well, maybe there is a reason to celebrate. . . .

"Satisfaction. That's what I got out of it," Shiva-Rose said, her expression determined.

"I'll drink to that." Alexis raised her tall water glass.

"I really can't believe what you did," Chloe told Shiva-Rose. "Seriously, you've got some willpower."

On the cab ride over to Max Brenner, Shiva-Rose had filled the girls in on the gossip: Mack had tried to cheat, give Shiva-Rose a head start on the challenge. But Shiva-Rose had refused to hear any of it, had gotten up and walked away.

"What Mack did was unfair," Shiva-Rose said softly. "He shouldn't have tried to tip me off."

"But how will it affect your relationship with him?" Chloe asked, a catch in her voice. "Do you even want a relationship?"

"I haven't thought that far," admitted Shiva-Rose. "And at least for tonight, I don't want to think about it."

Alexis raised her arm in the air, trying to get a waiter's attention.

Lindsay noticed they'd not been served yet. "That's odd," she commented. "The last time we were here, they were falling all over themselves trying to get to us."

Alexis stood up and signaled a passing waiter. "We're ready for some chocolate at this table," she called out.

He nodded at a pair of waitstaff huddled at the counter. "They'll be right with you," he said, and scurried away.

"Maybe they're holding a lottery," Alexis speculated with a grin. "The winner gets to wait on us."

"Guys?" Chloe spoke up, nervously folding her hands in her lap. "I have something to tell you."

"What's up?" Shiva-Rose asked, leaning forward.

Chloe cleared her throat. "I've made a big decision. I'm leaving the program."

Oh, my God.

Lindsay, for once in her life, was speechless.

It worked? It actually worked?

"Whaaat?" Alexis swiveled toward Chloe so quickly, she knocked her water glass over.

"You can't!" Shiva-Rose declared.

"I've made my mind up. Liam is more important to me than . . . this." A tear dropped down Chloe's cheek, and Lindsay was surprised to feel a pang of sorriness.

"Can we at least discuss?" Alexis pleaded.

Chloe dabbed at her eye with the corner of her napkin. "It's pretty simple. If I go home now,

I have a chance with Liam. If I stay, he goes."

"Did he say that?" asked Shiva-Rose, shocked.

"He didn't have to," Chloe said. "He's moving on."

"Unless you get there and stop him?" Shiva-Rose asked incredulously.

"Won't you break mama's heart by leaving?" Lindsay couldn't help herself. Hitting Chloe where it hurt had become such a fun sport. She'd actually miss her when she left.

"Please don't go," Alexis begged. "Not now. I mean, in a weird way, we've become friends." She eyed Lindsay. "Mostly. That counts for something, doesn't it?"

"I booked an airline ticket for tomorrow," Chloe sniffed. "I'm telling Victoria, then I'm out of here."

Alexis elbowed Lindsay. "Say something. If you ask her, she'll stay."

Lindsay opened her mouth, utterly unsure of what to do.

"Excuse me."

Lindsay looked up. The waiter Alexis had fawned over and nicknamed Tyson had materialized. It was about time. Only he didn't seem interested in taking the girls' orders. He focused on Alexis, who was still trying to get Chloe to change her mind.

"Did you not hear me?" Tyson raised his voice.

How rude! Lindsay almost said it. Then she noticed two brawny security-types standing over by the counter, watching them.

Alexis scrunched her forehead. Shiva-Rose and Chloe wore identical looks of alarm.

"My manager has asked to speak with you. Follow me."

"Me?" Alexis look dumbfounded. "Is it because I won?"

Shiva-Rose stood up. "Is there a problem?"

Chloe stood, too. "What's going on? Is there something I can help with? I'm—"

Lindsay couldn't stop herself. She bolted upright. "Do you even know who I am?"

"I don't care who any of you are," Tyson said evenly. "She's the one we have on our security tape. Not once but twice. Brazen, aren't you?"

Alexis looked so tiny, the only one still sitting. Her face had gone from flushed with joy to white with terror. Shiva-Rose placed a hand on Alexis's shoulder.

"I'm sure there's an explanation." Chloe pulled herself up to her full height, trying to look patrician, probably. Like that was going to help.

"What did you do, Alexis?" Shiva-Rose asked. "What did you do?"

"You came back?" That was all Lindsay could think of to say.

"I came back with Sh-Sh-Shane," Alexis stammered. "A few days ago."

"Yes, you did," said the now ominous-looking waiter. "So either you come quietly with me now, or I will call the police. . . ."

To Be Continued . . .

Read on for a teaser from Eye Candy, the next juicy read in the* America's Next Top Model™ *series!

They were all dressed in Kitty Lyon's creations.

And they all looked fabulous!

It was Friday night, an hour before the glittering launch party for Kitty Lyon's US fashion line. For the first time all week, the 14C girls couldn't have been more excited. They all felt as if they'd been instantly catapulted into the supermodel lifestyle, as if the world was their oyster.

Even Chloe was feeling somewhat pumped. It was hard not to, looking as glamorous as she did with her hair swept into a messy updo; her lips a pale, glossy pink; and her slim body poured into a strapless, flowy leopard-print dress.

Lindsay was rockin' the snakeskin mini, which she'd paired with a form-fitting white tank and white sky-high platforms.

Alexis had chosen a halter sundress in a shimmery blue batik pattern with chunky tribal-inspired jewelry.

Shiva-Rose, ever the practical one, went with the Kitty Lyons version of the little black dress — short, straight, spaghetti-strapped — which was accented with a wide tiger-print belt.

After swapping lip glosses and blushes and

taking at least a zillion giggly snapshots with their cell phones, the girls made their way downstairs. Parked outside the building was a party bus waiting to take them to Bungalow 8, which had been rented out specifically for the event. Victoria, Dan'yel, Annabelle, and Mack would already be there, in their dual capacities of partygoers-slash-chaperones, awaiting the girls' arrivals.

As the girls boarded the enormous nightclub-on-wheels, the driver stopped Lindsay. "Ms. Robinson," he said in a formal tone. "Ms. Devachan asked me to give this to you and to have you read it aloud to the girls once we're on our way."

Lindsay took the envelope he held out to her. When everyone was seated, and the bus pulled out into the traffic, Lindsay opened the envelope.

"Listen up everyone," she said, waving the letter to get their attention. "We've got another V-mail." She cleared her throat and read:

"Good evening, models. You are now on your way to your first official public appearance as fashion ambassadors of Top Model Prep."

"Oooh," called Erica, a brunette with cobalt-blue eyes who lived on the fifteenth floor. "We're, like, ambassadors!"

"It is imperative that you conduct yourselves accordingly," Lindsay read. "That is to say, you will behave in a professional manner at all times. You will be polite, you will be appropriate, and you will be respectful of others and of yourselves."

Lindsay paused to let the magnitude of the statement sink in, then read on.

"While we expect you to mingle with other guests, remember, the majority of these people will be strangers to you, and it is wise to be careful. You are all very attractive young women. Expect to be fawned over and flirted with. Boys will be boys, after all, but most of these boys are, in fact, grown men. Should you find yourself the recipient of any unwanted attention or in a situation that makes you even the slightest bit uncomfortable, please find me or one of the other instructors immediately. Having said that, I also understand that girls will be girls, and there is sure to be an abundance of handsome men in attendance tonight. We insist that you maintain your dignity at all times. There is to be no public displays of affection, no lewd dancing, and especially no leaving the party with anyone other than one of the TMP instructors. Barring an individual emergency, we will all depart together, as a group, at exactly midnight."

A chorus of groans rose up around the party bus.

"Midnight?"

"That's so early!"

"So much for this being the city that never sleeps!"

"Those are the rules, folks," said Lindsay, folding the letter back into its envelope. "I don't make 'em, I just read 'em."

The party bus pulled up to the club and the girls rushed to the windows to gape at the crowds gathered on both sides of the velvet ropes.

"Is that Kate Hudson?"

"Look, there's Zac Efron and Vanessa Hudgens. I love her dress."

"I see Heidi Klum. Man, I would kill for her legs!"

"Hey, who's that really old guy over there?"
"That's Mick Jagger."

"Oh, my God, my mother loves him."

"My grandmother loves him!"

The 14C girls were the last TMP students to enter Bungalow 8. By some unspoken agreement, they were going to do this together. They did not walk in single file with someone symbolically taking the lead, but marched forward, four abreast, shoulder to shoulder, slender curved hip to slender curved hip. And what a statement that made — like soldiers of fashion mustering their ranks, they exuded a united force of power, confidence, and glamour, while at the same time, each girl wore her unique beauty like a medal of honor, wielded it like a weapon.

And . . .

Heads . . .

Did . . .

Turn.

Cameras flashed and whispers rippled through the crowd.

"Who are they? They're gorgeous. They're fabulous."

Inside the club, the lights were soft, the music was loud, the outfits were outrageous, and the people were important. And the important people were looking at the girls of 14C!

Their entrance mission successfully accomplished, the girls gracefully parted company.